Inspiring Primary Curriculum De

Inspiring Primary Curriculum Design offers support and ideas for teachers, school leaders, teaching assistants and student teachers to develop their knowledge of the research related to curriculum design, giving specific and practical ideas to apply research in primary school contexts. This first book in the brand-new series 'Unlocking Research' combines practitioner expertise with world class academic research and reflects cutting-edge educational thinking from the only university-run primary school in the UK.

Co-written by practising teachers and research academics and drawing from a wide and diverse theoretical and research base, each chapter includes examples of how schools approached designing their own curricula; providing a route map of ideas and questions for readers to explore in their own contexts. The aim is to empower educational professionals in reclaiming the processes of curriculum design from evidence-informed foundations and to identify opportunities to be bold, innovative and imaginative.

Packed with innovative ideas and practical suggestions, this book highlights the importance of using research evidence to develop teachers' practice in the realities of their own classrooms and schools. This will be a key read for teachers, school leaders, teaching assistants and student teachers, especially those who recognise the important role of research in developing excellence in their practice.

James Biddulph completed his PhD at Cambridge University. He is a successful educator and the Headteacher of the first and only University Training School for Primary Education. Prior to being the Headteacher of the University of Cambridge Primary School (UCPS), he was the inaugural Headteacher of Avanti Court Primary in East London. He completed two Masters, one in Music and one in Educational Research during this time. Early on in his career he was awarded Outstanding New Teacher of the Year and gained Advanced Skills Teacher status.

Julia Flutter has worked in education research for over 20 years as a Research Associate at the Faculty of Education, University of Cambridge, where she has been focusing on collaborative approaches for improving classroom teaching. She was a director of the Cambridge Primary Review Trust, a not-for-profit organisation promoting excellence in primary education, and an Associate Editor for the internationally respected *Cambridge Journal of Education*. She was a contributing author and sub-editor to the Cambridge Primary Review final report, *Children, Their World, Their Education* (edited by Professor Robin Alexander and published by Routledge, 2010).

Unlocking Research
Series Editors: James Biddulph and Julia Flutter

Unlocking Research offers support and ideas for students and practising teachers, enriching their knowledge of research and its application in primary school contexts. Packed with imaginative ideas and practical suggestions, the series aims to empower teachers, teaching assistants and school leaders to take research-informed and principled approaches to making necessary changes in schools so that teaching and learning ignites the social imagination for 21st century educators and learners.

For more information about this series, please visit: https://www.routledge.com/Unlocking -Research/book-series/URS

Inspiring Primary Curriculum Design

Edited by James Biddulph and Julia Flutter

LONDON AND NEW YORK

First published 2021
by Routledge
2 Park Square, Milton Park, Abingdon, Oxon OX14 4RN

and by Routledge
52 Vanderbilt Avenue, New York, NY 10017

Routledge is an imprint of the Taylor & Francis Group, an informa business

British Library Cataloguing-in-Publication Data
A catalogue record for this book is available from the British Library

Library of Congress Cataloging-in-Publication Data
Names: Biddulph, James, editor. | Flutter, Julia, editor.
Title: Inspiring primary curriculum design / edited by
James Biddulph & Julia Flutter.
Description: Abingdon, Oxon; New York, NY: Routledge, 2020. |
Series: Unlocking research | Includes bibliographical references and index. |
Identifiers: LCCN 2020008591 | ISBN 9780367228330 (hardback) |
ISBN 9780367228385 (paperback) | ISBN 9780429277108 (ebook)
Subjects: LCSH: Education, Primary–Curricula–Great Britain. |
Curriculum planning–Great Britain.
Classification: LCC LB1564.G7 I67 2020 | DDC 375.00941–dc23
LC record available at https://lccn.loc.gov/2020008591

ISBN: 978-0-367-22833-0 (hbk)
ISBN: 978-0-367-22838-5 (pbk)
ISBN: 978-0-429-27710-8 (ebk)

Typeset in Bembo
by Deanta Global Publishing Services, Chennai, India

Contents

Contributors

James Biddulph
University of Cambridge Primary School

Jonathan Clarke
Hemingford Grey Primary School, Cambridgeshire

Penny Coltman
Faculty of Education, University of Cambridge

Lucy Downham
Peckover Primary School, Wisbech

Richard Dunne
Ashley Church of England Primary School, Walton-on-Thames

Julia Flutter
Faculty of Education, University of Cambridge

Kate Fox
Hemingford Grey Primary School, Cambridgeshire

Nitesh Gor
Avanti Schools Trust

Lisa Harford
St James' Church of England Primary School, Cheltenham

Phil Kirkman
Anglia Ruskin University

Mark Lacey
Diocese of Salisbury Academies Trust

Michelle Long
Dixon Academies Trust, Bradford

Emilie Martin
Ashley Church of England Primary School, Walton-on-Thames

Neil Mercer
Faculty of Education, University of Cambridge

Ana Mocanu
Faculty of Education, University of Cambridge

Mark Priestley
University of Stirling

Harriet Rhodes
Faculty of Education, University of Cambridge

Luke Robbins-Ross
Dixon Academies Trust, Bradford

Susan Lee Robertson
Faculty of Education, University of Cambridge

Luke Rolls
University of Cambridge Primary School

Graham Schweig
Christopher Newport University, USA

Caryn Smith
St James' Church of England Primary School, Cheltenham

Rachel Sutton
Peckover Primary School, Wisbech

Stephen J Toope
University of Cambridge

Jane Warwick
Faculty of Education, University of Cambridge

John-Mark Winstanley
Faculty of Education, University of Cambridge

Andy Wolfe
Church of England

Constantinos Xenofontos
University of Stirling

1

Curriculum making
Key concepts and practices

Mark Priestley and Constantinos Xenofontos

Introduction

It would appear – after a long hiatus spanning nearly 30 years – that curriculum is back on the agenda in England's schools. This observation does, of course, require some qualification. In one sense, curriculum has never gone away; reform of the school curriculum has been a preoccupation of successive governments, with policy characterised by tinkering – and occasionally larger scale overhaul – of the National Curriculum, which has continued to exert a major – some would say malign – influence on practices in schools. However, this is different to saying that the curriculum, as an object or field of study and a set of discourses subject to critical examination by education professionals, has been the focus of educational attention in England. We would suggest that this has not largely been the case, and that the field of curriculum studies – by both scholars and education professionals – has been in decline for some time. Some commentators have talked of a 'crisis in curriculum' (Wheelahan, 2010) in recent years, echoing earlier talk in the United States that the field had become moribund (Schwab, 1969). Such rhetoric is perhaps overstated; nevertheless, we would agree that the field of curriculum studies has been in the doldrums for some years in the UK (Moore, 2006; Manyukhina & Wyse, 2019). A major cause of this has been the influence of the National Curriculum, a good example of a teacher-proof curriculum (Taylor, 2013). In its various iterations, through tight and prescriptive regulation of content and even pedagogy (Hofkins & Northen, 2009), it has sought to reduce teachers from active curriculum makers to technicians tasked with delivering a predefined product. This is amply illustrated by one particular trend in recent years – the decline of the curriculum studies Master's degree. In the early 1990s, teachers were able to undertake Master's level programmes with a primary focus on curriculum at many universities; in 2019, only one such programme remains in the UK, and it is currently projected for closure. These trends have been accompanied by a decline in curriculum scholarship and the

1

retirement of key scholars in the field, and a distancing of curriculum scholars from the institutional settings (including schools) where curriculum is made and remade (van den Akker et al., 2013). A corollary of this has probably been the strengthening of a view amongst the teaching profession that curriculum scholarship is not relevant to the task of developing educational programmes in schools.

In the light of this apparent decline in curriculum studies, we therefore welcome signs that the field is experiencing something of a renaissance; 'a vigorous debate on the school curriculum with questions concerning curriculum design and implementation moving to the top of the educational research and policy agenda internationally' (Manyukhina & Wyse, 2019, p. 1). A notable trend has been the emergence worldwide of new forms of curriculum policy which explicitly reposition the teacher as an agent of curriculum change and active maker of the curriculum in local school settings (Priestley & Biesta, 2013). Examples of such development are found in Scotland's Curriculum for Excellence and the new Curriculum for Wales. This approach to curriculum policy has explicitly eschewed the detailed prescription of content – input regulation of the curriculum (Nieveen & Kuiper, 2012) – which has been a key feature of policy for much of the life-cycle of England's National Curriculum. The repositioning requires teachers to be more than simple implementers of policy, but instead as professionals who interpret, translate, mediate and enact policy through the exercise of professional judgement. Overall, such curricula have placed questions about curriculum, including curriculum design/development/making, firmly back into the orbit of practitioners.

To some extent, recent trends in England reflect worldwide trajectories, although there are some significant differences which would seem to militate against the development of the extended role of the teacher as a curriculum maker, as has been encouraged elsewhere in the world. Prominent amongst these has been the knowledge turn, following the election of the Conservative/Liberal Democrat coalition in 2010. The launch of England's revised National Curriculum by Michael Gove in 2012 represented a considerable divergence from international trends towards decluttering of content, and more autonomy in curriculum making – including selection of content – by teachers. Its prescription of content in core subject areas and the lack of specification in 'unimportant' non-core subjects (Alexander, 2012, p. 376), along with its lack of clear aims, have been heavily criticised as undermining curricular balance and coherence. According to Alexander (ibid.):

Since this contrast is reinforced by assessment requirements, with English, mathematics and science subject to national tests and 'some form of grading of pupil attainment', we can be reasonably sure on the basis of past experience that in a significant proportion of schools teachers will teach to the test and have scant regard for the rest.

Paradoxically, these ambiguities in curriculum policy seem to have opened up spaces for teachers to become more active and agentic curriculum makers. By encouraging the narrowing in the curriculum, about which Alexander warned, curricular policy has exposed the need for schools and teachers to be sites where curriculum questions are posed and addressed constructively. It is no longer the case – if it ever was – that schools can unproblematically 'implement' the government's curriculum product.

It is heartening to see, in this political context, that curriculum debate is firmly back on the agenda in schools. The recent emergence of the Ofsted Intent, Implementation, Impact (Harford, 2017) approach to curriculum planning is encouraging, as it explicitly requires schools to address curriculum questions. It acknowledges that curriculum is something that 'happens' at various levels of the system, it recognises the important role of teachers as translators of policy and significantly emphasises the importance of conceptual clarity. It recognises the importance of knowledge, something that has been 'downgraded' to some extent in curriculum policy developments elsewhere in the world (Young & Muller, 2010; Priestley & Sinnema, 2014). Nevertheless, despite these encouraging signs, there remains a need for a more nuanced approach to conceptualising and enacting curriculum. The Ofsted model remains limited in many respects; it is too linear and top-down, and replete with problematic language such as 'delivery' and 'offering', rather than 'experience' and 'development'; and there is too much focus on content, neglecting other curriculum practices, especially pedagogy and assessment, which are seen as not being part of the curriculum.

The remainder of this chapter will explore some of these issues, taking as its starting point the current debates about curriculum. To a large extent, these debates were foreshadowed by the Cambridge Primary Review (Alexander, 2009; Hofkins & Northen, 2009); this comprehensive approach to curriculum was perhaps published, however, at the wrong time to have the full impact it deserved. Given current debates about the importance of curriculum, we now seem to be at a more constructive juncture to critically examine the concepts and practices associated with curriculum, many of which were featured in the Review. The next section will explore the meaning of curriculum in more detail, especially examining critical concepts that should underpin the development of educational programmes in primary schools.

Curriculum concepts

It can be argued that effective curriculum making has to be underpinned by developed conceptual understanding by the curriculum makers (particularly practitioners); sense-making by teachers is suggested to be a key factor in the development of state-mandated, large-scale curriculum reform in systems perceived as successful, such as Finland (Pyhältö, Pietarinen & Soini, 2018). It is therefore useful to start this discussion with an attempt to define curriculum, which is a contested and often misunderstood concept. At a simple level, the curriculum simply means a course of study. The word is derived from the Latin word meaning racecourse or race, and has come to mean a general course, conveying the notion of going somewhere in a predefined direction. Indeed, this simple definition is one that is current in many schools, where the curriculum is seen largely as the glossy booklets that contain the content to be taught.

However, such a conception of curriculum is clearly inadequate for understanding the complex processes of schooling in today's society. It can reduce curriculum simply to content, and ignore practices such as assessment and pedagogy that need to be considered when the curriculum is developed in schools. A more sophisticated definition is clearly required, and there have been many attempts to provide one. For example, the *Dictionary of Education* (Rowntree, 1981) offers the following definition:

> [Curriculum] can refer to the total structure of ideas and activities developed by an educational institution to meet the learning needs of students, and to achieve desired educational aims. Some people use the term to refer simply to the content of what is being taught. Others include also the teaching and learning methods involved, how students' attainment is measured and the underlying philosophy of education.

Scotland's Curriculum for Excellence, in line with this more holistic view, states that the curriculum is 'the totality of all that is planned for children and young people throughout their education' (Scottish Government, 2008). There are many other approaches in the literature highlighting the complexities of what curriculum comprises. Robitaille and Dirks (1982), for instance, discuss three levels of curriculum: the intended (a set of formal documents specifying what the relevant regional/national education authorities plan), the implemented (the interpretation of the intended curriculum by teachers and the actual implementation taking place in the classroom, based on teachers' beliefs, knowledge and experiences) and the attained (knowledge, understanding, skills and affective variables learners actually acquire as a result of teaching). These ideas were later used as a model of what curriculum is in the Second International Mathematics Study (SIMS) and have subsequently influenced the work of many educationists, who, in turn, provided more detailed/refined typologies.

Such definitions are helpful in that they provide a broad conception of the education that occurs in schools. However, this sort of broad definition can also be confusing, as the term curriculum comes to mean different things to different people. For these reasons, it is necessary to be clear about the various facets that make up the curriculum, and the ways in which these facets link together and interact in practice. One way in which this has been addressed is to identify how curriculum fits with other components of education, such as assessment and pedagogy, while seeing them as conceptually distinct practices. For example, Bernstein's (1977) famous formulation of the three message systems of schooling – curriculum, pedagogy and assessment – is one such attempt to show how these practices interrelate. However, this typology comes with dangers if it allows education professionals to consider such issues separately, and we would advocate instead an approach which requires all such questions to be addressed as part of a holistic method of engaging with the development of educational practice.

With the above in mind, we offer an alternative, holistic definition of curriculum: *the multi-layered social practices, including infrastructure, pedagogy and assessment, through which education is structured, enacted and evaluated.* Such a definition moves us beyond thinking of the curriculum as a product which needs to be delivered or implemented. Instead, it views curriculum as something that happens – or which is done – differentially across different layers of the education system, as the curriculum is *made* in different institutional settings. Put differently, and to paraphrase Bernstein (1990), the curriculum is contextualised in policy, and recontextualised as it is [re]made (interpreted, translated, enacted) in different schools. This definition of curriculum also requires us to consider how different curricular practices interrelate, and how the curriculum relates to educational purposes, students and the wider social context, for example:

- Questions relating to curriculum for what, by whom … and for whom?
- The necessity of considering context, including the 'hidden curriculum', when engaging in local curriculum making.
- The importance of teacher professional development, bearing in mind Stenhouse's (1975) aphorism that there can be no curriculum development without teacher development.
- The role of system dynamics as barriers to and drivers of curriculum making.
- The need to take an inclusive and holistic approach, which takes account of the perspectives and experiences of traditionally marginalised groups.

A regular response to the argument that curriculum needs to be viewed holistically as described above is the refrain 'but that is not curriculum, it is pedagogy (or assessment)'. A couple of examples will illustrate why we should resist such thinking, as the curriculum is made in schools. We offer these examples on the assumption that how one learns is as significant as what one learns in shaping the intellect. The first example relates to the development of new subject content, and has been a commonplace issue in Scotland as Curriculum for Excellence has unfolded (Fenwick, Minty & Priestley, 2013). Many schools have discussed the possibility of developing new courses, in the spirit of the new curriculum, to integrate teaching in the sciences and social studies. In practice, what has emerged has been the development of modular programmes that continue to teach the constituent subjects separately, the sole difference being that a single teacher is responsible for teaching all of the subjects, instead of different subject specialists. This has defragmented the student experience by reducing the number of teacher contacts per week, but has arguably reduced quality in teaching, and has done little to make connections across the curriculum. The new practices have been constrained by timetabling arrangements, the availability of teaching resources and limited prevailing understandings of integrated curricula. In Scotland, these decisions have been left for schools to make, with a comparative absence of national level resources. Our point here is that it is not possible to make decisions about changing content without consideration of the infrastructure (support, guidance, resources, timetabling) that facilitates the new approach. The second example relates to pedagogy. A Scottish school introduced cooperative learning as a pedagogical approach widely deemed appropriate for Curriculum for Excellence (Minty & Priestley, 2012). In this case, the initiative was unsuccessful, largely because of existing structural arrangements (the 50 minute period made extended activities difficult) and the physical characteristics of the school (desks bolted to the floor and facing the front made group work all but impossible). Again, our point is that decisions about what has been traditionally seen as the curriculum (i.e. content) are shaped by many other factors, and these need to be taken into account when curriculum making.

In contrast to the view outlined here, curriculum is more frequently narrowly conceived as knowledge/content. We do not deny the importance of knowledge here, and would agree with the Cambridge Primary Review, which rejects arguments that:

> process is all that matters, and that knowledge is ephemeral and easily downloaded after a Google search. Knowledge matters because culture matters .... In fact, culture is what defines us.
>
> *(Hofkins & Northen, 2009)*

Instead, we would argue that a conception of curriculum as simply knowledge is potentially reductive. As well as often failing to acknowledge the interconnectivity of curricular practices, as outlined above, there is a tendency to reduce knowledge to subjects. As Whitty (2010, p. 34) points out, 'knowledge is not the same as school subjects and school subjects are not the same thing as academic disciplines'. Such thinking runs the risk of subjects becoming the ends of education, rather than, as they should be seen, as a particular means of organising knowledge in the curriculum. Subjects have a tendency to become set in stone, and we have seen over the years how some subjects have established themselves on the curriculum as unchallengeable entities, supported by powerful subject associations (Goodson & Marsh, 1996). A corollary of this has been the development of gaps in the curriculum as society changes (do we adequately cover social, political and environmental issues in the current school curriculum?) and overcrowding as new subjects are sometimes bolted on to address the issue of gaps (e.g. citizenship in the secondary – but not primary – National Curriculum). This incremental approach does not lend itself to a coherent curriculum. Moreover, there are alternative rigorous approaches to teaching disciplinary knowledge that are inter-disciplinary in nature, rather than being framed as traditional subjects (for example, see Beane, 1997; Wall

& Leckie, 2017). Addressing these problems requires a shift in thinking – the key question is not 'what subjects do we teach?', but instead 'what knowledge, skills and attributes are required for educating the human to be a participant in a complex and pluralistic modern society?'. And crucially, this includes the questions 'who are the learners?', and 'how do we get there?', which further raise questions around the issues discussed above, concerning pedagogy, assessment, provision and support infrastructure. As Biddulph and Flutter suggested in the Introduction, to some extent, curriculum planning can be approached in the same way as organising a journey: a) Where do we want to go? (knowledge, skills, attributes); b) who is coming to the trip? (knowing the learner); c) how do we get there? (pedagogy) and d) what did each traveller get from the journey? (assessment).

A related issue, which has characterised debate around the curriculum in England, but less so elsewhere in the UK, concerns the development of spurious dichotomies. These include knowledge versus skills, children versus subjects and 'traditional' versus 'progressive'. These dichotomies have become prevalent in recent times, undermining the assertions of many who advocate a view of curriculum based solely on knowledge, that curriculum is a separate issue from pedagogy, as they regularly conflate so-called 'traditional' curricular structures based on subjects with 'traditional' teaching methodologies. According to Hofkins and Northen (2009, p. 41), 'there is an easy way to eliminate these facile, but dangerous, dichotomies'. This is to "simply substitute 'and' for 'not' and 'versus'" (ibid.). Put simply, a good teacher will draw upon a range of teaching methodologies regardless of whether they are deemed to be traditional or progressive, and will value the acquisition of knowledge. Similarly, John Dewey (1907), regarded by many as the father of progressive education, explicitly rejected what he saw as the false dichotomy of knowledge and process, emphasising the importance of the 'accumulated wisdom of the world'. In both cases, the key criterion for selection should be fitness-for-purpose.

This brings us to the discussion of educational aims and purposes. A particular strength of the Cambridge Primary Review was its advocacy of a curriculum rooted firmly in educational aims, and guided by clear principles. Many modern curricula (e.g. Curriculum for Wales) are similarly grounded in a clear expression of aims and purposes, which are intended to drive practice. In effect, a statement of aims addresses the question 'what are schools for?'. Conversely, the various iterations of England's National Curriculum have been at best weakly rooted in aims. As Alexander (2012, p. 372) so neatly put it, this is the:

> Mrs Beeton approach – first catch your curriculum, then liberally garnish with aims – is not the way to proceed. Aims must be grounded in a clear framework of values – for education is at heart a moral matter – and in properly argued positions on childhood, society, the wider world and the nature and advancement of knowledge and understanding. And aims should shape curriculum, pedagogy, assessment and the wider life of the school, not be added as mere decoration.

A clear statement of aims in curriculum policy is only the starting point. It should be accompanied by systematic sense-making by teachers. Clarity of purpose is a necessary prerequisite for constructive and purposeful curriculum making. This requires time to be set aside for structured and ideally collaborative discussions about curricular aims and purposes, their meaning and their implications for practice.

Thinking of curriculum as a social practice, with due consideration of aims and subsequent development of practice, then leads us to consider the role of the curriculum makers – teachers – and how their professional agency as curriculum makers might be developed. The term capacity is sometimes used to refer to teacher agency. This usage is in line with modern political discourses around teaching – for example the oft-expressed truism that the quality of a system cannot exceed the quality of its teachers. However, this sort of thinking is at best incomplete, and at worst can be misleading, leading to the misallocation of resources, and reductionist thinking that places the responsibility – and the blame – for curricular failure at the door of teachers. Alexander (2012, p. 380) offers a more nuanced account of capacity, suggesting that:

> 'curriculum capacity' refers to the human and other resources that a school is able to command in two areas:
>
> ■ relating to the aims, scope, structure, balance and content of the curriculum as a whole;
> ■ relating to the detailed planning and teaching of individual curriculum subjects, domains or aspects.

This view suggests that 'capacity' – or more accurately 'agency', as capacity is only one aspect of teacher agency – is dependent on the availability of resources. The ecological understanding of teacher professional agency (Priestley, Biesta & Robinson, 2015) takes this thinking a step further. Personal capacity (e.g. professional skills and knowledge, and teacher dispositions and beliefs) is only part of the story; agency is dependent as well on the resources available to teachers, and shaped by the social context within which, and by means of which they act. Agency is not therefore something innate to an individual, but is achieved in particular, and always unique situations, through an interplay of personal qualities and contextual conditions. Therefore, if we are serious about enabling teachers to become effective curriculum makers, then we need to not only raise their professional capacity – we also need to address their cultural and structural working conditions. Even the highest calibre teachers can be disabled by their environment. The ecological understanding of agency thus suggests that system actors (including policymakers and school leaders) need to focus less on excellent teachers and more on excellent teaching.

This raises important questions about the extent to which an educational system allows teachers the 'discretionary space' to approach curriculum as a social practice. This is linked to some extent to how centralised/decentralised an educational system is. In the case of the Republic of Cyprus (a highly central-ised system), for instance, teachers do not have significant discretionary space to 'deviate' from the prescribed agenda, despite policy rhetoric about autonomy. In this sense, they are not allowed to be curriculum makers. In the case of Scotland, teachers are, at least in theory, given more freedom and space to take decisions, and yet system dynamics, for example accountability mechanisms, often preclude this (Priestley, Biesta, Philippou & Robinson, 2015; Kontovourki, Philippou & Theodorou, 2018; Xenofontos, 2019); moreover, many teachers lack the profes-sional knowledge and confidence to make use of the space afforded (Priestley, Biesta & Robinson, 2015).

Curriculum process

Over time, curricula have been developed around content, often delineated into traditionally configured subjects. Proponents of these approaches have argued that subjects offer distinct advantages in relation to framing disciplinary knowl-edge, particularly when closely aligned to particular disciplines, and that they offer induction into communities of practice formed around disciplines and/or subjects. As we have noted, however, this approach comes with problems, notably a conflation of knowledge and subjects, and a tendency for subjects to become the ends rather than the means of the curriculum. Recently, national curricula have tended to eschew this approach, instead framing education around competencies and learning outcomes, often highly specified and set out as lin-ear ladders of progression. The tendency for such frameworks to drive teaching through assessment, becoming effectively tick lists of criteria, has been well documented, along with associated issues around strategic compliance, workload and bureaucracy (e.g. Minty & Priestley, 2012). A more constructive approach seems to be the process model of curriculum, grounded in clear educational purposes, and paying attention to the processes then necessary to achieve them. The Cambridge Primary Review adopts this approach, with its suggestion of focusing on 12 aims that can be adopted to provide structure and coherence across every aspect of primary education.

According to Kelly,

> the starting point for educational planning [in a process curriculum] is not a consideration of the nature of knowledge and/or the culture to be transmit-ted or a statement of the ends to be achieved, whether these be economic or behavioural, but a concern with the nature of the child and with his or her development as a human being.
>
> *(Kelly, 1999, p. 78)*

The starting point is educational aims through, as previously noted, critical sense-making by teachers of curriculum policy and critical engagement with the

9

question 'what are schools for?'. Such engagement involves balancing nationally agreed priorities in policy with local imperatives, and also, as emphasised, inevitably involves professional judgement as the official curriculum is made – interpreted, translated and enacted – in local contexts. Curriculum making entails three linked processes, as teachers derive the following from curricular aims:

- *Selection of content*: deriving appropriate knowledge (including skills and dispositions) to meet curricular purposes. We reiterate here that a process approach does not preclude the acquisition of what has been called powerful knowledge (e.g. Young & Muller, 2010).
- *Selection of method*: structuring education programmes to ensure that pedagogy is coherent and fit-for-purpose, building in regular opportunities for assessment.
- *Provision*: organising the curriculum to ensure coherence and progression, accounting for links between different domains of knowledge where applicable (e.g. subjects, cognate areas of learning, interdisciplinary approaches).

We conclude this section with two points. First, and often neglected in curriculum making, it is essential that teachers identify barriers and drivers to their curriculum making, and (importantly) address them through concrete actions. As the chapters which follow will demonstrate, these actions include approaches for enhancing professional knowledge, setting up new structures and engaging in discussion with external partners. Second, schools should not neglect the hidden curriculum (Hargreaves, 1982). We do not have space here to discuss this in detail; suffice to say, for example, that there is little point in developing a curriculum, based around the voice of children and young people, if the discipline practices of the school undermine this, or if the school's culture marginalises their voices. Similarly, establishing a vocational strand to the curriculum, or a co-curricular programme, will be limited in effectiveness, if the predominant message is that certain subjects (Mathematics, English, Science) are more important. It is helpful to make a school's values explicit in its curricular documentation and policies, but they need to be lived values too.

A summary of key points

In closing this chapter, we would like to recapitulate two key points that readers might find useful to take with them as they read on to the next pages.

- Firstly, in talking about the curriculum, we suggest that we should move away from definitions that approach the concept as a product. We propose an alternative definition of curriculum: the multi-layered social practices through which education is structured, enacted and evaluated. Such an approach empowers teachers as curriculum makers and emphasises the important role of teacher agency in the process of change. On the one hand, highly centralised educational systems do not always allow teachers the discretionary space to act as curriculum makers. On the other hand, highly decentralised systems may, in theory, allow teachers the freedom and space to act as such, yet without necessarily providing them with the tools and opportunities for professional development that would facilitate constructive curriculum making.

■ Secondly, for curriculum to be an effective set of social practices, systemic changes need to take place. Those changes should not only allow teachers the space to act as curriculum makers and decision takers; they should also address issues regarding the perceptions of some school subjects as more important than others, and the extent to which the voices of learners and their respective cultural communities can be heard, are valued and are considered.

References

Alexander, R. (Ed.) (2009) *Children, Their World, Their Education: Final Report and Recommendations of the Cambridge Primary Review*, 1st edition. London: Routledge.

Alexander, R. (2012) Neither national nor a curriculum? *Forum*, 54(3), 369–384.

Beane, J.A. (1997) *Curriculum Integration: Designing the Core of a Democratic Education*. New York: Teachers College Press.

Bernstein, B. (1977) *Class Codes and Control, Towards a Theory of Educational Transmissions, Volume 3*. London: Routledge and Keegan Paul.

Bernstein, B. (1990) *The Structuring of Pedagogic Discourse: Class Codes and Control, Volume 4*. London: Routledge.

Dewey, J. (1907) Waste in education. In: J. Dewey (Ed.), *The School and Society: Being Three Lectures by John Dewey Supplemented by a Statement of the University Elementary School* (pp. 77–100). Chicago: University of Chicago Press.

Fenwick, A., Minty, S. & Priestley, M. (2013) Swimming against the tide: A case study of integrated social studies. *The Curriculum Journal*, 24(3), 454–474.

Goodson, I.F. & Marsh, C.J. (1996) *Studying School Subjects: A Guide*. London: The Falmer Press.

Harford, S. (2017) Curriculum: intent, implementation and impact. Development work for the new inspection framework. Slide presentation available online at: https://www.slideshare.net/Ofstednews/educationfest17 [accessed 03.04.2020]

Hargreaves, D. (1982) *The Challenge for the Comprehensive School: Culture, Curriculum and Community*. London: Routledge.

Hofkins, D. & Northen, S. (2009) *Introducing the Cambridge Primary Review*. Cambridge: Faculty of Education, University of Cambridge.

Kelly, A.V. (1999) *The Curriculum: Theory and Practice*. 4th edition. London: Sage.

Kontovourki, S., Philippou, S. & Theodorou, E. (2018) Curriculum making as professionalism-in-context: The cases of two elementary school teachers amidst curriculum change in Cyprus. *The Curriculum Journal*, 29(2), 257–276.

Manyukhina, Y. & Wyse, D. (2019, in press) Learner agency and the curriculum: a critical realist perspective. *The Curriculum Journal*, 30(3), 223–243.

Minty, S. & Priestley, M. (2012) *Developing Curriculum for Excellence in Highland Schools: A Report on the Qualitative Findings for the Highland Council and the Scottish Government*. Stirling: University of Stirling.

Moore, A. (2006) Introduction. In: A. Moore (Ed.) *Schooling, Society and Curriculum* (pp. 1–14). Abingdon: Routledge.

Nieveen, N. & Kuiper, W. (2012) Balancing curriculum and freedom in the Netherlands. *European Educational Research Journal*, 11(3), 357–368.

Priestly, M. & Biesta, G.J.J. (Eds.) (2013) *Reinventing the Curriculum: New Trends in Curriculum Policy and Practice*. London: Bloomsbury Academic.

Priestley, M., Biesta, G.J.J., Philippou, S. & Robinson, S. (2015) The teacher and the curriculum: Exploring teacher agency. In: D. Wyse, L. Hayward & J. Pandya (Eds.), *The SAGE Handbook of Curriculum, Pedagogy and Assessment* (pp. 187–201). London: SAGE Publications Ltd.

Priestley, M., Biesta, G.J.J. & Robinson, S. (2015) *Teacher Agency: An Ecological Approach*. London: Bloomsbury Academic.

Priestley, M. & Sinnema, C. (2014) Downgraded curriculum? An analysis of knowledge in new curricula in Scotland and New Zealand. *The Curriculum Journal*, 25(1), 50–75.

Pyhältö, K., Pietarinen, J. & Soini, T. (2018) Dynamic and shared sense-making in large-scale curriculum reform in school districts. *The Curriculum Journal*, 29(2), 181–200.

Robitaille, D. & Dirks, M. (1982) Models for the mathematics curriculum. *For the Learning of Mathematics*, 2, 3–21.

Rowntree, D. (1981) *A Dictionary of Education*. London: Harper & Row.

Schwab, J.J. (1969) The practical: A language for curriculum. *The School Review*, 78(1), 1–23.

Scottish Government (2008) *Building the Curriculum 3: A Framework for Learning and Teaching*. Edinburgh: Scottish Government.

Stenhouse, L. (1975) *An Introduction to Curriculum Research and Development*. London: Heinemann Educational.

Taylor, M.W. (2013) Replacing the 'teacher-proof' curriculum with the 'curriculum-proof' teacher: Toward more effective interactions with mathematics textbooks. *Journal of Curriculum Studies*, 45(3), 295–321.

van den Akker, J., Kuiper, W. & Hameyer, U. (Eds.) (2013) *Curriculum Landscapes and Trends*. Amsterdam: Springer.

Wall, A. & Leckie, A. (2017) Curriculum integration: An overview. *Current Issues in Middle Level Education*, 22, 36–40.

Wheelahan, L. (2010) *Why Knowledge Matters in Curriculum: A Social Realist Argument*. London: Routledge.

Whitty, G. (2010) Revisiting school knowledge: Some sociological perspectives on new school curricula. *European Journal of Education*, 45(1), 28–44.

Xenofontos, C. (2019) Primary teachers' perspectives on mathematics during curriculum reform: A collective case study from Cyprus. *Issues in Educational Research*, 29(3), 979–996.

Young, M. & Muller, J. (2010) Three educational scenarios for the future: Lessons from the sociology of knowledge. *European Journal of Education*, 45(1), 11–27.

2

Considering the possibilities

James Biddulph and Julia Flutter

"Would you tell me, please, which way I ought to go from here?"
"That depends a good deal on where you want to get to".
"I don't much care where —"
"Then it doesn't matter which way you go".

Alice and The Cheshire Cat in Alice's Adventures in
Wonderland by Lewis Carroll (1865:26)

Introduction

As we saw in Chapter 1, in recent decades the curriculum debate has become
a maelstrom of polarised argument and changing policy, leaving many teachers
and senior leaders wondering which direction, or directive, they should follow
next. As the Cheshire Cat wryly observes, before setting out on a journey we
have to know where we're heading to and so addressing this question has to
be our starting point. The destination for our curricular journeys is of para-
mount concern and must be determined by the values, aims and purposes we
have in mind. Before we venture further, though, we need to be clear about
what we mean when we talk about a *curriculum*. Definitions vary and reflect
differing perspectives on what is being encompassed in the word. The current
National Curriculum in England offers this definition, for example, which
frames the idea of a curriculum firmly within the parameters of content and
accountability:

> The national curriculum is a set of subjects and standards used by primary and
> secondary schools so children learn the same things. It covers what subjects
> are taught and the standards children should reach in each subject.
>
> *(DfE, 2019)*

In contrast, the Scottish National Curriculum, *Curriculum for Excellence*, provides a broader definition which extends beyond the boundaries of subjects and

measured outcomes to envisage the curriculum as a vehicle through which to achieve a clearly articulated set of aims:

> Curriculum for Excellence is designed to achieve a transformation in education in Scotland by providing a coherent, more flexible and enriched curriculum from 3 to 18. The term curriculum is understood to mean – everything that is planned for children and young people throughout their education, not just what happens in the classroom.
>
> *(Education Scotland, 2019)*

This definition moves us beyond the notion of curriculum as content to include the conceptualisation of curriculum as a 'lived experience' involving the delineation not only of subjects, skills and capacities that students should acquire but also an awareness and consideration of the social, cultural and affective dimensions of learning. However, both of these officially prescribed definitions suggest that a curriculum is an essentially 'given' entity and are based on the premise that teaching and learning must be framed within a designated set of affordances and constraints which will lead to achieving the desired educational outcomes.

Beyond these official perspectives, researchers, practitioners and educational theorists have taken their own stances in addressing the question of what a curriculum is and what it entails. In the 1970s, influential educationalist Professor Lawrence Stenhouse emphasised the connection between ideas and practice, which he argued should be embodied in the notion of a curriculum. Connecting the rationale for *what* is being taught with *how* it is to be realised within the classroom, Stenhouse summarised his perspective by suggesting that: "A new curriculum expresses ideas in terms of practice and disciplines practice by ideas" (1975:107). Rather than a framework of *content*, under Stenhouse's viewpoint, the curriculum is to be seen as an ongoing *process* involving discussion, reflective thinking and continual revision, and therefore a curriculum is always tentative and open to change. American author Thomas Popkewitz affirmed this argument that the curriculum should be considered as a work in progress but cautioned that whatever ideas we have in mind and wish to implement, enacting these plans will be likely to produce unexpected outcomes: "The history of the curriculum is one in which theories are never realized in the manner they are intended. There are always unintended, unanticipated, and unwilled consequences as theories are put into social action" (1988:69).

Throughout this book, we adopt a definition of the word curriculum that is similarly provisional and discursive. We will be considering curricular possibilities through not only the lenses of content and pedagogy but across the full spectrum of what teachers and schools plan and do to achieve their aims for children. In the chapters which follow, we hear about the journeys others have taken in creating their own primary school curricula and we hope that through engaging with our travellers' tales you will discover new possibilities and questions to inform and inspire your own curricular decision-making. At the end of this chapter, you will also find a set of prompt questions which can be used to support discussions about curriculum design with staff, parents, governing bodies and children. And, indeed, developing an enquiring mindset and asking questions is key to deepening your understanding of curricula matters. We begin, however, by considering where we want our curriculum journeys to take us and look at the aims we have in mind for primary education which represent the destinations we are striving towards.

Heading out

In many ways, the process of curriculum design involves similar decision-making steps to the planning of any journey; as suggested earlier on, we need to be clear about the aims and purposes which give us our direction of travel and we need to find ways to realise these objectives. The curriculum design journey must begin with delineating our aims and purposes because, as the Cambridge Primary Review points out, this is an essential starting point:

> The first step in shaping a school's curriculum is to determine the educational purposes for which it stands and the aims that it will pursue.
> *(Cambridge Primary Review Trust, 2014:10)*

Between 2007 and 2010, the Cambridge Primary Review team (led by Professor Robin Alexander) carried out a large-scale, comprehensive review of evidence on primary education in England and other countries. As part of the Review's evidence-gathering, a call was made for people to submit their ideas and opinions about primary education, and the Cambridge Primary Review team posed a set of questions to help frame these submissions (Alexander, 2010). In relation to the aims and purposes of primary education, the Review's questions were:

- What is primary education for?
- Taking account of the country and the world in which our children are growing up, to what individual, social, cultural, economic and other circumstances and needs should this phase of education principally attend?
- What core values and principles should it uphold and advance?
- How far can a national system reflect and respect the values and aspirations of the many different communities – cultural, ethnic, religious, political, economic, regional, local – for which it purportedly caters?
- In envisaging the future purposes and shape of this phase of education, how far ahead is it possible or sensible to look?

The thousands of responses that contributed into the Review's extensive dataset revealed an interesting and wide-ranging spectrum of perspectives and reflected the differing values, priorities and beliefs of those who submitted their thoughts. In analysing this evidence, the Review's research team were able to discern some recurrent themes across these viewpoints, which included the following concerns: the importance of literacy and numeracy but as part of a broad, balanced curriculum; the need for education to address social and emotional wellbeing and to nurture the 'whole child'; addressing the persisting problem of social disadvantage; questions surrounding faith and spirituality; balancing individual and societal needs; questions relating to community, cultural and citizenship matters; global awareness and concern about the future (Alexander, 2010). As well as opinions, the Review also brought together national and international research evidence on the aims and purposes of primary education and on the basis of its accumulated evidence, the Review's final report proposed a model of aims based on three dimensions: aims relating to *the individual*; aims relating to *the self, others and the wider world*; and aims relating to *learning, knowing and doing* (see Figure 2.1).

It is important to note that the Review's model is not offering a tick list or recipe of things that should go into the curriculum mix but rather it is suggesting an interconnected, coherent set of aims that, in combination, are intended to help teachers and schools to fulfil their obligations to each and every child, to society and to the global community. These aims are not only integral to the Review's curriculum model, as we shall see later on, but the Review argues that they are also integral to pedagogy, assessment and everything that happens within a school's life. In Chapter 3, we will hear more about the implementation of these ideas as we discover how they have influenced curricular decision-making at the University of Cambridge Primary School in Cambridge.

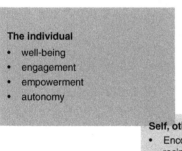

The individual
- well-being
- engagement
- empowerment
- autonomy

Self, others and the wider world
- Encouraging respect and reciprocity
- promoting interdependence and sustainability
- empowering local, national and global citizenship
- celebrating culture and community

Learning, knowing and doing
- exploring, knowing, understanding, making sense
- fostering skill
- exciting the imagination
- enacting dialogue

Figure 2.1 The Cambridge Primary Review aims. (Based on: The Cambridge Primary Review Trust/Pearson, 2014)

The Cambridge Primary Review's approach is only one possibility for thinking about aims for primary education, of course, and there are many others that we could consider – and there are differing lenses we could use in focusing on the question of aims. We could explore the question using a sociological framework to explore aims for society in terms of power relationships, social equality and social justice, for example. Professor Michael Young, and others, have taken such an approach and are concerned with fostering a "knowledge-rich" curriculum that affords access to "powerful" specialist forms of knowledge with the aim of achieving social justice for all. Inspired by Michael Young's work, Carolyn Roberts, head teacher of Thomas Tallis School in Greenwich, has written the following guidance for her staff:

A knowledge-driven school

To the staff

We are the people who offer powerful and shared knowledge to the nation's children. That knowledge comes from centuries of learning, and from the research of universities and subject associations. It is powerful because it enables children to interpret and control the world; it is shared because all our children should be exposed to it. It is fair and just that this should be so. It is unfair and unjust when children are offered poor quality knowledge which fails to lift them out of their experience.

Here are ten things to remember.

(1) Knowledge is worthwhile in itself. Tell children this; never apologise that they need to learn things.

(2) Schools transmit shared and powerful knowledge on behalf of society. We teach what they need to make sense of and improve the world.

(3) Shared and powerful knowledge is verified through learned communities. We need to keep in touch with universities, research and subject associations.

(4) Children need powerful knowledge to understand and interpret the world. Without it, they remain dependent upon those who have it.

(5) Powerful knowledge is cognitively superior to that needed for daily life. It transcends and liberates children from their daily experience.

(6) Shared and powerful knowledge enables children to grow into useful citizens. As adults, they can understand, cooperate and shape the world together.

(7) Shared knowledge is a foundation for a just and sustainable democracy. Citizens educated together share an understanding of the common good.

(8) It is fair and just that all children should have access to this knowledge. Powerful knowledge opens doors; it must be available to all children.

(9) Accepted adult authority is required for shared knowledge transmission. The teacher's authority to transmit knowledge is given and valued by society.

(10) Pedagogy links adult authority, powerful knowledge and its transmission. We need quality professionals to achieve all this for all our children.

(Carolyn Roberts quoted in Young, 2014:10)

Other sociologists have argued that, whilst focusing on social justice is important and worthwhile, we should take a more holistic perspective on the aims and purposes of education and consider these through a multidimensional approach. Aims that centre on fostering certain forms of knowledge or sets of skills are therefore taken as being only part of the curriculum picture and other aims are equally significant, both for society and the individual. Professor Gert Biesta, for example, suggests that educational aims should be considered across three domains: *qualification, subjectification* and *socialisation*. Biesta describes *qualification* as:

> the transmission and acquisition of knowledge, skills and dispositions. This is important because it allows children and young people to "do" something – it qualifies them. This "doing" can be very specific, such as in the field of vocational and professional education, or it can be conceived more widely, such as in general education that seeks to prepare children and young people for their lives in complex modern societies.
>
> *(2015:4)*

However, as Biesta goes on to explain, education is about more than knowledge, skills and dispositions and it also embraces other aspects of human life and endeavour including cultural, professional, political and other facets as the *socialisation* dimension (Biesta, 2015). Biesta's domain of *subjectification* refers to the way in which: "children and young people come to exist as subjects of initiative and responsibility rather than as objects of the actions of others" (Biesta, 2015:4).

Within the confines of this introductory chapter, we can do no more than scratch the surface of these complex and contrasting arguments, and touch base with a few of the key ideas that are currently leading debates on the aims and purposes of the curriculum. What is important, however, is to bear the Cheshire Cat's warning in mind and, before we set out on our journey to design a curriculum, we need to think carefully about our desired destinations.

From aims to practice

The broad, national aims of state education are largely laid down by governments and each society's expectations about what it means to be educated. We saw earlier that the Cambridge Primary Review gave recommendations about what this could be; however, the Review's final report also suggested that localised decisions about the aims and purposes of an individual school's curriculum should be permitted within the framework of a national curriculum to address the needs of the specific community the school serves. This important, local dimension has been a particular focus for the University of Cambridge Primary School (UCPS) and Avanti Schools (discussed in Chapter 8) which, as new schools, had to articulate their aims and purposes prior even to children joining the schools. In the case of UCPS, the process involved in curriculum decision-making was responsive to the growing community served by the school and a number of 'sounding' activities were undertaken (these steps are documented in Chapter 3). It is important, therefore, in considering how we move from aims to practice that our decision-making is guided not only by the big picture of national policy but also by the closer context within and surrounding the school.

It is also important to note that this journey, from aims to practice, like Alice's fall through the rabbit's warren, will evolve and bring about new ways of thinking, believing and being; it will be confusingly frustrating at times, with the pressures of external points of view and the numerous stakeholders to consider. The various chapters in this book exemplify these differing journeys. We will hear the tales of our fellow travellers on the curriculum-making journey; some are experienced practitioners and researchers whose stories are based on many decades in classrooms and schools, whilst others have only recently embarked on their curricular adventures and share their travelogues with us, both positive and negative.

In helping you to navigate through your own journey, we would like to offer a route-map which you may wish to follow. There are, of course, many alternative approaches for considering what a curriculum could be, what it could mean for teachers and how it is understood and lived by the children. In the following section, we share three principles as starting points: (1) the importance of questioning, (2) the use of creative strategies to develop professional discourse and (3) the potential of using theoretical lenses.

The importance of questioning

Developing a professional discourse about curriculum is essential, in our view, to ensuring it is enacted fully within the classroom. In building a curious professional community, a number of signposting questions can be asked:

- What do we want our communities to be like in 50 years' time and what do we need to teach now to make those communities a reality?
- How do we want our children to engage in the world in 50 years' time?
- What will our children remember of their schooling in 50 years' time? And what will they forget?
- How will we know our curriculum was effective?
- What does 'being prepared for secondary school' mean?
- What does 'being prepared for life' mean?

- What is important for our local community? Immediate concerns and long-lasting ones?
- Where are the inequalities in our community?

Questions like these can be used during staff meetings to form the basis of discussions with senior leaders. Initial answers to the questions can lead to new lines of enquiry, building a mindmap of possible directions of travel. The experience of one of the authors asking these questions was profound: insights and openings arose as educators and communities discussed what it meant for them to live in the community, to learn in the community and to live beyond the community. Staff began to pinpoint the (metaphoric) locations and sites of interest along the curriculum-designing journey.

Creative strategies: images and metaphors

The second of our suggested starting points involves the creative use of images and metaphors as a means of generating thought and discussion on the purposes and aims of the school. This strategy can then be used to support the process of defining a coherent set of purposes and aims for the school designed curriculum. Images can be found, often random and unrelated to education, with the aim of catalysing philosophical discussion. As part of professional development sessions, the whole teaching community are invited to select images and to connect it with this question, "What is the curriculum we want for our children at [name of the school]". Following these discussions, the images chosen by each member of staff, can be collated and displayed on a staffroom wall (see Figure 2.2, image is from the author's school).

In the author's school, this strategy proved valuable in prompting new ideas and directions for curriculum decision-making. After the initial discussion with images being selected, further thinking was promoted over the following weeks through using 'post-it' notes to add comments, explanations or disagreements to the staffroom wall display, and the curriculum visioning lived on for a number of weeks. Referring to Figure 2.3, examples of additional comments included:

- Strong roots and foundations to represent different paths children will take
- Allow children to know and live by their rights
- Bringing children out of themselves
- Individual journey; everyone is different
- Grounded/soil/flourishing/coaching/team

What would this mean for the curriculum design and implementation? How would we assess what is valued? In what specific ways can children 'be brought out of themselves' in the day-to-day business of teaching and learning? The view of individualisation also comes through in these added comments, but how could this be realised in an organised school curriculum?

Figure 2.2 Visioning the curriculum – a creative task

Figure 2.3 Reflections on a new journey

Senior leaders in the author's school then took the vision board and collated what had been documented into a coherent statement that was shared again with the team. This iterative process took some time but as the White Rabbit explained to Alice, "the hurrier I go, the behinder I get". Schools often feel compelled to rush in and grasp the latest (often externally generated) agenda, idea and policy but we advocate for getting 'behinder', allowing ideas to gestate and be mulled over during staff breaks so that poignant and profound concepts can be brought to the surface. This gradual process, as we will see in the chapters which follow, results in a shared ownership of the aims and purpose of not only the school but the vision behind the curriculum design.

The use of theory

Our third suggesting starting point is the use of theory. Teaching is inherently a philosophical and sociological pursuit, although in the busyness of the day-to-day, there is limited time to consider it as such. However, we encourage appropriate use of different theoretical lenses through which to explore the work of educators in schools and classrooms. In so doing, it strengthens a curriculum design and, through such enquiry, can give courage and confidence to teachers and school leaders that their design has intellectual substance. Here we present a brief overview of the theoretical perspective offered in the work of Pierre Bourdieu as an example.

Bourdieu was an influential sociologist and his work resonates and remains a useful lens through which to explore education practices. As with almost everything in education, his views are contested and held to question. However, his so-called 'thinking tools' have helped the authors in considering questions about not only *what* is taught in the curriculum, but also the pedagogy through which the curriculum is taught and experienced. His theory shines a light on the possible assumptions those in power have and exert on the decisions on curriculum design.

Bourdieu's theoretical 'thinking tools' are attractive for questioning the purposes of curriculum design because they try to uncover "the most deeply buried structures of the different social worlds that make up the social universe" (Bourdieu, 1996:1) – for our purpose, the deeply held structures in schools that translate into the ways schools work, and how teachers teach. The interrelated terms of *habitus*, *field* and *capital* could provide us with ways to make sense of the complex and multilayered processes within schools and in classrooms. For example, *habitus*, which is more than habits of a particular social group, refers to certain 'ways of life' because of a set of values, principles and agreed ways of doing things. How often have we heard teachers and school leaders say, "this is how we do things in our school"? We do not always see our own *habitus* because it is just the way we are, act and engage in the world; our truth is our own truth.

To illustrate further, it is true to say that the vast majority of primary teachers have been successful at school, have achieved academically, have first if not further degrees and, therefore, have the ability to determine what happens in school now that they are employed as teachers. Having gone through the current educational system, we know how the education game works and are good at playing that game. Without bringing the use of theory into our thinking, the danger is that we continue to propagate what worked best for ourselves, with the old adage that teachers teach in the ways that they like to learn. And this then determines what we value within the 'social fields' of schools, what Bourdieu calls *capital*.

There are external ways of defining capital (like graded examinations that give access to the next level of education such as A-Levels that gain entrance to university) but individual teachers define the capital of their classrooms in the same way that senior leaders define the capital of the wider school context. So, we problematise our position by asking more questions: What do we value? Quiet children? Chatty children? Independent learners or compliant learners? Do we value manners and good behaviour? Or do we nurture outspoken children? What types of relationship do we nurture with our children? Our answers to these questions are value-laden decisions that define the *capital* within a classroom and school community. Children soon learn what the teacher values. Teachers learn what the senior leaders value. Headteachers learn what the government and governors value. It becomes cyclical: the *capital* determines the *habitus* which reinforces the definition of the *capital*. This then becomes the practice within the *social field* of school; it becomes how educators teach and behave. It becomes how children achieve or fail. It becomes how we do things in school and it affects how we design the curriculum.

Bourdieu's own research evidences and reconfirms social inequalities and disadvantages that are reinforced by education systems; those in power (teachers and senior leaders) inadvertently, through the 'blindness' of their own *habitus*, reaffirm what the society values (the *capital*) – and notions of the hidden curriculum are born. These matters are complex and difficult to resolve. There is value, however, in asking more questions to foreground the assumptions we make about the children, their families and the values of diverse communities and indeed about ourselves as educators. One way to do this is in confronting assumptions through creative professional development (as can be seen in the second book of this current series (Biddulph and Cariss, 2020), to give unusual professional experiences for teachers and teaching assistants that nudge them out of their expected comfort zones, in doing so, giving the sense of a fish out of water. So, using Bourdieu's theory, in continuing to ask questions:

- What is it we value in and for ourselves?
- What do we value in our work and in our schools?
- What messages, both explicit and implicit, will we be teaching our children?
- What are our assumptions about children, childhood and growing up?
- Where are the gaps in our own educational experience?
- When did we not learn something easily?
- How will a curriculum design give opportunities for diverse experiences of learning that push teachers out of their own learning comfort zones?

Whilst we have but briefly introduced the thinking tools of Bourdieu's theoretical framework, in essence we advocate for the use of educational philosophy and/or sociological concepts to help staff teams consider their work in more rounded and principled ways; to use suitable theoretical lenses through which to view, affirm and/or reconsider their positions, values and decisions. Our discussion questions at the end of this chapter signpost the reader to possibilities for such theoretical gazing. In the end, you may discard these lenses, but they will invite new thinking and open new possibilities.

Journeying onwards

Maxine Greene talks about education as a journey that requires us to plunge in; to choose; to disclose; to move, which will eventually bring a sense of mastery (Greene, 1971) – that is, until the next journey starts. The road ahead may seem daunting. If the reader is preparing to set out on their curriculum design journey, it will be easier to purchase a curriculum from a reputable publisher and adapt it to their school, but it is unlikely that this will be the best possible curriculum for their children, their staff and their community. For those who have already embarked, the activities shared in this book are invitations to develop further conversations about the curriculum. What we have found, and what is articulated throughout this book, is that whilst the curriculum-making journey is fraught with intellectual and practical challenges, the meandering, upward struggles through overgrown pathways lead to new opportunities of discovery – and eventually lead to a curriculum design which is principled, coherent and belongs to those who teach and learn every day in each school community.

Further discussion questions

- What do children currently learn in the primary phase?
- Do the current national curriculum and attendant foundation, literacy, numeracy and primary strategies provide the range and approach of what children of this age really need?
- What should children learn during the primary phase?
- What kinds of curriculum experience will best serve children's varying needs during the next few decades?
- Do notions like 'basics' and 'core curriculum' have continuing validity, and if so, of what should 21st century basics and core for the primary phase be constituted?
- What constitutes a meaningful, balanced and relevant primary curriculum?

(Alexander and Flutter, 2009:4)

References

Alexander, R. and Flutter, J. (2009) *Towards a New Primary Curriculum: A Report from the Cambridge Primary Review. Part 1: Past and Present.* Cambridge: University of Cambridge Faculty of Education.

Alexander, R. (Ed.) (2010) *Children, Their World, Their Education: Final Report and Recommendations of the Cambridge Primary Review.* London: Routledge.

Biesta, G.J.J. (2015) What Is Education For? On Good Education, Teacher Judgement and Educational Professionalism, *European Journal of Education*, 50(1), 1. doi: 10.1111/ejed.12109.

Bourdieu, P. (1996) *The State Nobility: Elite Schools in the Field of Power.* Cambridge: Polity Press.

Cambridge Primary Review Trust (2014) *Primary Curriculum 2014: Developing an Outstanding Curriculum in Your School.* London: Pearson.

Carroll, L. (1865) *Alice's Adventures in Wonderland.* London: MacMillan and Company.

Department for Education (2019) *The National Curriculum.* London: Department for Education.

Education Scotland (2019) *Curriculum For Excellence.*

Greene, M. (1971) Curriculum and Consciousness. *Teachers College Record*, 73(2), 253.

Popkewitz, T.S. (1988) Knowledge, Power: A General Curriculum. In: *Cultural Literacy and the Idea of General Education, 87th Yearbook of the National Society for the Study of Education, Part 2*, eds. Ian Westbury and Alan C. Purves. Chicago: University of Chicago Press, p. 69.

Stenhouse, L. (1975) Defining the Curriculum Problem, *Cambridge Journal of Education*, 5(2), 104–108.

Young, M. (2014) The Curriculum and the Entitlement to Knowledge. A Talk Given at a Seminar Organised by Cambridge Assessment Network on Tuesday 25 March 2014. Magdalene College, Cambridge. http://www.cambridge assessment.org.uk/Images/166279-the-curriculum-and-the-entitlement-to-knowledge-prof-michael-young.pdf [accessed 30.1.2019].

3

Nurturing compassionate citizens of the future
Weaving together pedagogy and curriculum

Penny Coltman and Luke Rolls

Introduction

We need to contemplate the future when we think about education in the present. We must acknowledge that the world in which our young learners will find themselves is likely to be a very different one from the present and the challenges they will face are yet unknown. We must ask what kind of people we want our children to become and how can we ensure they are able to face these challenges. In an increasingly turbulent world with issues of mental health, inequality, the corruption of democracies and a lack of willingness to embrace diversities frequently dominating headlines, it becomes even clearer that young people need to be equipped with a securely embedded set of skills, qualities and values which will help them to steer through the challenges and complexities of life. As well as arguing that this understanding should inform the curriculum content of what we teach, this chapter will discuss the ways in which we teach this, drawing upon established research literature. At the University of Cambridge Primary School (UCPS), we identified three hallmark pedagogies which appear to hold considerable potential for fostering learning autonomy (which we argue is vital for young people to grapple with the diversities of the 21st-century world). These 'golden threads' of oracy and dialogue, playful enquiry and habits of mind cannot be so easily separated from the 'what' of the curriculum when our curriculum aims are held in mind. In order to create truly compassionate citizens who develop both knowledge and academic excellence alongside positive dispositions as learners, our hope is that we nurture warm-hearted human beings. The *how* is as important as the *what*. But to start with, we must consider the *why*. Why are we doing what we are doing?

Our schools

Prior to our school opening, many hours were spent discussing key questions around the aims, values and ambitions of the school (Gronn & Biddulph, 2016). With the opportunity of a blank canvas for a new and unique 'university training school', a number of questions were posed:

- What was our vision for the school's pupils as future citizens?
- How could we enhance both children's learning and their wellbeing?
- How could we help to develop the critical thinking skills, resilience, courage, empathy, imagination and creativity needed to produce the craftspeople, doctors, mechanics or visionaries of the future?
- How do we balance knowledge-rich content with life-important skills?

The school was founded with influence from the Cambridge Primary Review (Alexander, 2010). Based at the Faculty of Education, University of Cambridge, the Review was carried out between 2006 and 2010 and was the most comprehensive review of primary education undertaken since the report of the Plowden committee published in 1967 (CACAE, 1967). A multitude of sources representing the widest possible representation of all involved in, or concerned with, primary education contributed to the Review. Although effective learning in maths and English was unsurprisingly a recurring theme of the submissions made to the Review, many made reference to the need for primary education to address the needs of the 'whole child'. Attributes such as joy, curiosity, interpersonal skills and enthusiasm were perceived as desirable foundations for the future. One parent's submission is especially pertinent in the context of this chapter:

> I do not relish being looked after in my older years by a generation, all of whom have level 5 in their SATs and 5A* GCSEs, but who will not be nice to me or each other and who will not value or seek to invest in relationships which hold communities and ultimately society in place.
>
> *(Alexander, 2010, pp 184–185)*

The two aspirations of academic excellence and an ethos of developing social and emotional competences are, however, by no means mutually exclusive. Indeed, a desire to nurture and develop compassionate citizens who will make a positive contribution to their local and global worlds is at the core of the UCPS curriculum. The UCPS curriculum embedded these aims within pedagogical approaches informed by a substantive body of recent research.

A purposefully designed curriculum

We have drawn on the extensive research evidence on pupil voice (Rudduck & Flutter, 2004). This has demonstrated the importance of fostering children's capabilities for making sense of the complex world in which they live through hearing their voices and empowering them to make and express reasoned decisions. Consequently, our curriculum aims to develop children's skills for discussing and challenging diverse positions respectfully and compassionately, nurturing discussion to consider diverse views about the world and how we should live in it. We actively promote critical thinking so that children question assumptions about truth and knowledge. For example, how do we know that Christopher Columbus 'discovered' America? Did he? Who told the story of his discovery? Which voices are missing? Why are they missing? In understanding the globalised communities in which we live, there is a need for children to learn with the diversities that exist in their local and global communities. Inspired by the words of Lord Williams (then Rowan Williams, Archbishop of Canterbury), quoted in the Cambridge Primary Review final report, UCPS committed to embracing diversity at school at local, national and global levels.

> If you're going to be a decision-making citizen, you need to know how to make sense and how to recognise when someone is making sense ... that there are different ways of making sense, different sorts of questions to ask about the world we're in, and insofar as those questions are pursued with integrity and seriousness they should be heard seriously and charitably.
>
> *(Lord Williams, 2008; quoted in Alexander, 2010, p 13)*

The enabling space of our curriculum

To promote the development of compassionate, articulate citizens for now and the future, we drew recognition that the ways in which we engage with children informally and formally determines how the principles are enacted and 'lived out'. In the UK, the Warwick Commission Report (2015) argued that our education systems should be creative learning landscapes, infused with possibility spaces (Burnard et al., 2017). Similarly, we have worked to develop enabling spaces for curriculum and pedagogic possibilities to arise; spaces that are collaborative, foster agency, communality and engender trust. Building from *Learning without Limits* (Hart et al., 2004) and *Creating Learning without Limits* (Swann et al., 2012), the enabling space of the school is anchored by the guiding values of *empathy*, *respect*, *trust*, *courage* and *gratitude*.

A new built space: the Learning Street

Built with a larger corridor (which we call 'the Learning Street'), the Learning Street is an extended shared space running between the classrooms of the school which allows for large and small-scale activities, shared between classes, enabling children to work independently or in groups on self or teacher-directed activities. The space is designed so that children have opportunities to make autonomous choices about their learning and playful enquiry, conditions that appear to promote high levels of self-regulated learning (Meyer & Turner, 2002). Learning Street tasks do however have structure around them; walking through them, a visitor would see the children applying the knowledge, skills and vocabulary that they have developed (and been taught) in the classroom, be supported in co-operative learning tasks by the presence of 'talk agreements' and guided reflection. These are accompanied by explicit teaching and defining what high-quality outcomes look like. Behind the physical environment and learning tasks are the invisible norms of school values, relationships, shared expectations, learned enjoyment and motivation. Indeed, it appears that the development of key indicators of play, language and self-regulation are dependent on emotionally warm, positive and purposeful social climates (Burke et al., 2016, Swann et al., 2012; Whitebread & Coltman, 2016).

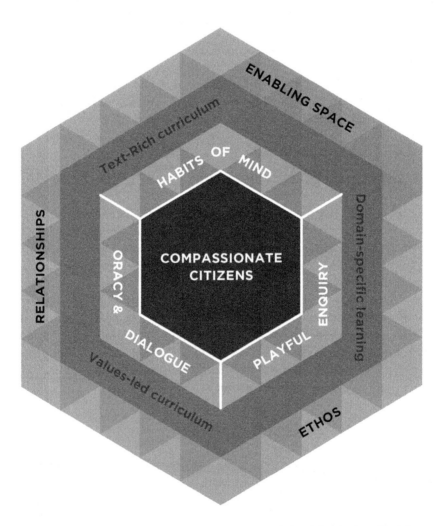

Figure 3.1 The University of Cambridge Primary School Curriculum Model

It is this interaction between the physical environment, the explicit nurturing of our school values and the relationships forged that create the 'enabling space' (Biddulph, 2017). Three 'golden threads' of habits of mind, oracy and dialogue, and playful enquiry were synthesised as pedagogical hallmarks through which to bind the curriculum together. When intertwined effectively with curriculum content, they appeared to hold significant potential for developing autonomous learners who are articulate, confident and able to express their views respectfully and intelligently; and who are curious, creative and playful in ways that deepen their knowledge and understanding of the world.

The representation of our curriculum (Figure 3.1) shows how different aspects of the curriculum framework form an inextricable matrix, with the interdependency of the elements being the foundation of the model's success. At the centre is the focal aim of nurturing compassionate citizens, with the inner layer representing the three golden threads, held together by an outer band of contexts for learning. These contexts enable core values to be understood through learning experiences that are meaningful and relevant to children: through the use of high quality text-rich learning, through domain-specific learning, cross-curricular learning and through ensuring that the guiding values of the school are explicitly modelled and discussed (Biddulph et al., 2017).

Golden thread: habits of mind

The ability of children to manage their own behaviours and emotions is a key part of self-regulation, a process increasingly recognised as pivotal in developing effective learning. As children learn how to learn, they make secure connections between success, effort and the deployment of appropriate strategies. The complex interplay between motivation, social and emotional factors and a child's ability to think about knowledge and thinking (metacognition) is thus now widely accepted as central in influencing performance and structuring memory (Whitebread, 2000).

Martha Bronson, working in the United States of America, put forward an innovative model of developing self-regulation in childhood, focusing on emotional, social, cognitive and motivational aspects and demonstrating how such factors are inextricably linked with learning (Bronson, 2000). Social aspects of self-regulation are very much concerned with the ways in which children gradually learn to be able to make and maintain friendships, to co-operate with others, and to resolve social problems independently of adults. Current research suggest that these social abilities are crucially dependent on children's developing 'theory of mind' i.e. their understanding that others have minds like their own, and may have quite different ideas, thoughts and feelings. Known in the literature as 'mastery orientation', there is research to suggest that a crucial precursor to motivation in young children is a feeling of control and of confidence in their own abilities. This appears to lead to foster a development of the resilience to take risks, learn from mistakes and enjoy challenges (Schunk & Zimmerman, 2008). Bronson (ibid) concluded that even very young children are astonishingly capable of voluntary self-regulation, an assertion supported by work such as that of the Cambridgeshire Independent Learning (CIndLe) project. Thirty-two foundation stage settings, representing both pre-school and reception class practitioners and children, contributed to this study with outcomes that have since been replicated in a significant number of countries (Whitebread & Basilio, 2012).

A key outcome of the CIndLe project was a checklist of relevant behaviours, observable in a classroom setting, which teachers could use to record children's self-regulatory development. Examples of emotional self-regulation frequently observed included the ability of children to recognise emotions in themselves and others, with children becoming increasingly aware of their own and others' emotions; an attribute fundamental to the development of emotional self-control and empathy. Signs of emergence of these emotional skills are evidenced as children help and comfort others, share and take turns independently, engage in co-operative activities negotiating how to carry out a task and resolve social problems with peers (Whitebread et al., 2005). Monitoring the frequency with which such behaviours were observed enabled teachers to refine their own pedagogical practices and to focus on the support of individuals.

There is evident resonance with the work of psychologists Art Costa and Bena Kallick who identified 16 psychological attributes and problem-solving skills important in supporting the learning process (Costa & Kallick, 2008). They coined the name 'habits of mind' to describe these attributes which mostly concern aspects of emotional and motivational self-regulation. Amongst them, they include reference to empathy, referring to the ability to put oneself in another person's shoes and to listen to their thoughts, ideas and feelings, and they include the notion of managing impulsivity: remaining calm and considering options. In their publication, Costa & Kallick (ibid) referred to these attributes as 'Habits of Mind' and identified six dimensions: value, inclination, sensitivity, capability, commitment and policy. They suggest that progression through these dimensions will develop in children the lifelong disposition to draw upon these behaviours when confronted with problems with consequently more successful outcomes.

Recognising the importance of developing these self-regulatory habits to promote effective learning, the University of Cambridge Primary School has sought to engage teachers in creatively embedding these into practice. Staff work together to plan for a learning environment that will capture children's imaginations and an ongoing enquiry into developing pedagogical approaches that aim to create self-regulated learning. With the aid of careful and sustained teacher modelling, children acquire and extend the language to enable them to talk about their learning, discussing for example what might have been a 'tricky point' in a lesson or task and what helped them in coming to their own and shared reflections about a key aspect of learning.

Golden thread: oracy and dialogue

In a world that is increasingly interconnected, complex communication skills are widely recognised as invaluable characteristics of productive and intercultural citizens (Autor, Levy & Murnan, 2003). It is therefore essential that a school curriculum enables the potential for learners to develop an ability to articulate their ideas and through active listening engage in 'inter-thinking' where they can build on the ideas of their own and others (Alexander, 2017). This kind of talk in which children listen to each other engaging with ideas, share relevant knowledge and justify their ideas and reasoning is known as 'Productive' or 'Exploratory' forms of dialogue (Howe & Abedin, 2013). Through several cycles of Lesson Study and teacher practitioner research, a number of key points from the dialogue research have become woven into pedagogy and curriculum at the University of Cambridge Primary School. Some of these shared school practices are summarised in Figure 3.2.

Firstly, it became clear that in order for children to engage in exploratory talk, it was essential that they saw a genuine purpose in any activities suggested by their teacher. Through appropriate challenges in their subject learning, they needed to specifically develop collaborative learning skills (Luckin et al., 2017) and assimilate shared understandings of 'rules for talk'. These included norms such as reaching a shared agreement, challenging and building on the ideas of others respectfully, distributing talk equitably amongst the group and having a positive attitude about learning within a group. As well as coming to naturalise these, learners needed specific opportunities to plan, reflect honestly and set goals together in the aim to create 'caring, collaborative, critical and creative' interactions (Phillipson & Wegerif, 2016). It was these dialogic skills in the classroom that underpinned the efficacy of dialogic approaches such as *Philosophy for Children*, empowering learners to create and discuss their own questions and change their minds through using their peers as effective instructional resources (Educational Endowment Foundation, 2015). Using the oracy framework (Millard & Menzies, 2016) allowed the school to evaluate which strands of dialogue were being purposefully developed in pupils across the curriculum. For example, a focus on the physical oracy strand was supported by weekly sessions with an instructor from the London Academy of Music and Dramatic Art (LAMDA) who expertly taught children to use their body and voice effectively. Within subject areas such as English and Geography, linguistic strands of oracy could be brought out. In reading sessions, vocabulary relating to the foundation subject learning was taught through several strategies such as 'dual-coding', contextualising language, using sentence stems, displaying vocabulary and metacognitive reflection opportunities. For example, in responding to the prompt 'how could a child labour employer sleep at night?', one child built on the idea of another friend to answer, showing a development towards using more advanced language: "I

Figure 3.2 Oracy and Dialogue School Strategies

don't think they could sleep because they would feel guilty for **employing** a child. They just **recruited** a child and **endangered** them by putting them in bad **conditions**".

Golden thread: playful enquiry

It is widely recognised that children experiencing some feeling of being in control of their environment and their learning is fundamental to them developing confidence in their abilities, and their ability to respond positively to setbacks and challenges (Goswami, 2015). In play, children set their own tasks, which may or may not be goal oriented. Sometimes the pleasure in a playful activity is gained through engaging with and exploring a process, with no particular end in mind. Children spontaneously set themselves challenges in their play and, given a choice, will often choose a task which is more challenging than one which an adult might have thought appropriate. Providing children with achievable challenges, and supporting them so they can meet them, is a powerful way to encourage positive attitudes to learning, and the children's independent ability to take on challenging tasks (Whitebread & Coltman, 2016).

It seems play also links closely to developing values. A key attribute of compassion is the ability to show empathy, to put oneself in another's shoes and see issues from another's perspective. This is very much related to social aspects of self-regulation in which children gradually learn to be able to make and maintain friendships, to co-operate with others and to resolve social problems independently of adults. Research suggests that such social abilities are crucially dependent on children developing a secure 'theory of mind', an understanding that others have minds like their own and so may have different thoughts and views (Wellman, 1988; Whitebread, 2000). This ability to consider the views of others is one of the cognitive skills greatly supported by imaginative role play, or 'socio-dramatic' play. This type of play is now recognised as one which offers intense challenge to children, requiring a high degree of self-regulation. 'Becoming' another in a role play scenario requires children to consider the possible responses that might be made by their character together with the gestures, voice and language they might use. Children must show an awareness of, and follow, the social rules of the context and character. The impact of pretence play in terms of developing deductive reasoning and the self-regulation of 'impulsive' behaviour has been shown repeatedly (Whitebread & Jameson, 2010). Working with children in special schools, O'Connor and Stagnitti (2011) found that children who engaged in socio-dramatic play were less likely than others to be socially disruptive and became more socially connected than those from a control group.

As children immerse themselves in pretend play, they create a context for learning which is real and meaningful to them as boundaries between reality and imagination become blurred and irrelevant. This notion of play and 'real' everyday experiences as equally valid meaningful contexts to young children will be confirmed by anyone who has observed a conversation between a child and a hand-held puppet. An imaginary context can be every bit as real for young children as a trip to the supermarket or an outing to the park (Tyrell, 2001; Coltman, 2006).

The school has worked to create a playful curriculum where children are given opportunities to explore and apply their learning through play. An over-arching topic is introduced each term which provides a focus for children's learning, and it is through each topic that different themes can be explored in imaginative and creative ways, allowing children to deepen their understanding in ways that best suit them. For example, in a topic on sustainable fashion, the challenges on the Learning Street served to provide rich formative assessment opportunities for children to independently apply learning from the classroom. Children had been faced with the consequences that disposable consumer fashion had on the environment in the polluted rivers next to clothes factories and in the devastating impact that cotton farming had on the Aral Sea. These ethical issues resonated with the children and they were motivated to learn each week in a group and then independently in a learning task that related to positive social action. On one station, children could be seen writing and preparing the posting of letters to high-street brands to ask how ethically sourced their clothes were. On another, a group of children would talk in the 'philosophy nook', recording video-logs debating whether 'fast-fashion' was a necessary evil. The computing-focused area housed a green screen and photography 'studio' where children could dress up and create video campaign logs around the social issues of fashion. Another station held a resourced sewing area for children to consolidate their sewing skills through various practice tasks for a classroom design and technology project they were engaging with. Teachers came to appreciate why this more independent learning time was a highlight in the week for children who reported back feeling a sense of agency that playful enquiry brought and used this to develop curiosity of a subject they were genuinely interested in. For acquiring knowledge around the fashion topic, explicit teaching was key but for enabling children to apply, play with and be creative with the knowledge they had gained, a degree of learning that involved choice and challenge was also valuable and appeared to foster longer-term aims of learning autonomy (James et al., 2007).

Weaving the threads: curriculum *in practise* and *as practice*

At UCPS, we initially experimented with both an immersive curriculum and a model of traditional weekly slots for different subjects; we found both to be problematic. Evenly dividing the curriculum into weekly lessons across all subjects was extremely difficult to timetable without inadvertently creating fragmented learning experiences. Equally, immersion subject learning where history for example would be taught for one or two weeks at a time left too long a gap between other subjects and so lacked coherence. We moved to using a flexible framework of selecting curriculum major and minor 'spotlight' subject areas grouped by half-termly learning progressions as well as identifying which curriculum areas required daily scheduling, such as physical exercise, singing and mindfulness. Other core and foundation subjects could be mapped with vertical progression across the school. It was notable, however, how lacking and sparse curriculum guidance materials and research were in supporting such planning and a large disparity in the materials available between subjects. Progression in learning to meet specified national curriculum outcomes were worked with as starting points, and mapped over the weeks to give each subject a spotlight focus so that children had the opportunity to go into depth in the unique 'lens' on the world that different subjects capture. This first stage of mapping the curriculum coverage laid out a coherent wider curriculum journey for children through the school in each academic year and progression of subject areas between years. This had positive implications for teacher workload; by removing top-level planning, teachers could be enabled to focus on the detail of sequencing the learning journey rather than spending considerable amounts of time on mapping coverage. The overview document given to teachers provided them with a starting point with suggested ideas but importantly also included the autonomy to bring their own knowledge and experience to decisions about how to design the learning sequence. From here, teachers in their planning teams and consulting with outside expertise, could use this base information to create more detailed week by week journey maps to set out learning outcomes. They would work backwards from these to plan the broken-down knowledge, concepts, skills and values needed to meet the desired endpoint. The framework in Figure 3.3 outlines the process of the medium term learning sequence planning from this starting point.

Reflections and development

In designing a curriculum, we need at the core, to understand its purposes: why are we doing it? What are we doing? How are we doing it? We need to consider what we want children to learn, how they might learn it, what space they will do it in, what will characterise their relationships and what knowledge, qualities and 'ways of being' such interactions will enculturate. While it is impossible to know exactly what the future will hold for our learners, principles can serve us well; alongside knowledge, does the enacted curriculum foster moral, human values, intelligence, warm-heartedness, collaborative and intercultural dispositions towards others? What we realise through our own enquiry into curriculum design is the core need for subject, curriculum and pedagogical development to be more closely aligned with ongoing professional development activities. Some of these themes arise in *Unlocking Research: Reimagining Professional Development* (Hargreaves & Rolls, 2020). In reflecting back over our process, and looking forward to the ongoing development of our curriculum, a number of points come to mind.

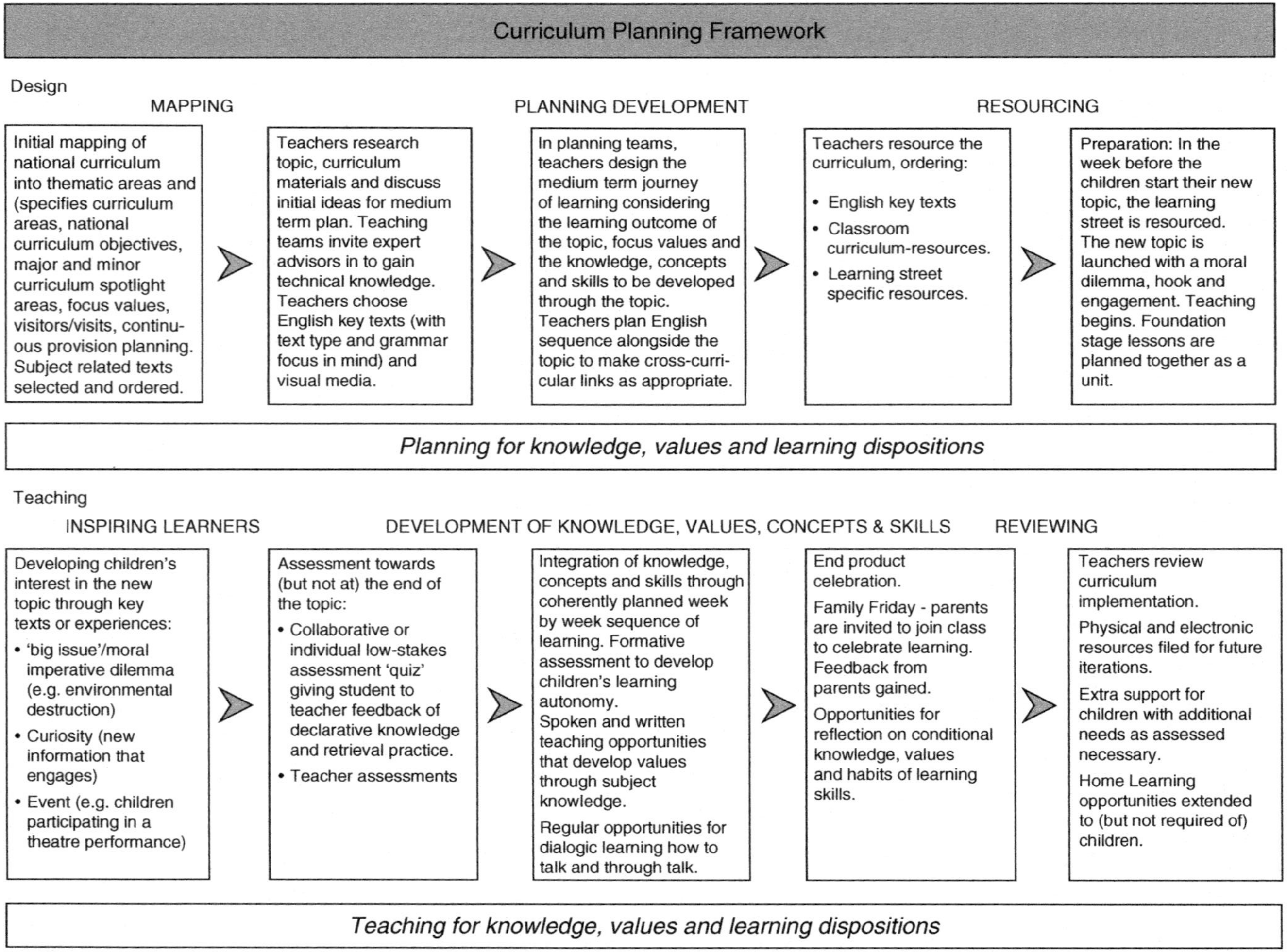

Curriculum Planning Framework

Design

MAPPING

Initial mapping of national curriculum into thematic areas and (specifies curriculum areas, national curriculum objectives, major and minor curriculum spotlight areas, focus values, visitors/visits, continuous provision planning. Subject related texts selected and ordered.

PLANNING DEVELOPMENT

Teachers research topic, curriculum materials and discuss initial ideas for medium term plan. Teaching teams invite expert advisors in to gain technical knowledge. Teachers choose English key texts (with text type and grammar focus in mind) and visual media.

In planning teams, teachers design the medium term journey of learning considering the learning outcome of the topic, focus values and the knowledge, concepts and skills to be developed through the topic. Teachers plan English sequence alongside the topic to make cross-curricular links as appropriate.

RESOURCING

Teachers resource the curriculum, ordering:

• English key texts
• Classroom curriculum-resources.
• Learning street specific resources.

Preparation: In the week before the children start their new topic, the learning street is resourced. The new topic is launched with a moral dilemma, hook and engagement. Teaching begins. Foundation stage lessons are planned together as a unit.

Planning for knowledge, values and learning dispositions

Teaching

INSPIRING LEARNERS

Developing children's interest in the new topic through key texts or experiences:

• 'big issue'/moral imperative dilemma (e.g. environmental destruction)
• Curiosity (new information that engages)
• Event (e.g. children participating in a theatre performance)

DEVELOPMENT OF KNOWLEDGE, VALUES, CONCEPTS & SKILLS

Assessment towards (but not at) the end of the topic:

• Collaborative or individual low-stakes assessment 'quiz' giving student to teacher feedback of declarative knowledge and retrieval practice.
• Teacher assessments

Integration of knowledge, concepts and skills through coherently planned week by week sequence of learning. Formative assessment to develop children's learning autonomy.
Spoken and written teaching opportunities that develop values through subject knowledge.
Regular opportunities for dialogic learning how to talk and through talk.

REVIEWING

End product celebration.
Family Friday - parents are invited to join class to celebrate learning. Feedback from parents gained.
Opportunities for reflection on conditional knowledge, values and habits of learning skills.

Teachers review curriculum implementation.
Physical and electronic resources filed for future iterations.
Extra support for children with additional needs as assessed necessary.
Home Learning opportunities extended to (but not required of) children.

Teaching for knowledge, values and learning dispositions

Figure 3.3 Curriculum Planning Cycle

Systems: As an education system, we need a much more coherent set of curriculum support materials. There is little sense in teachers creating similar resources across the country or haphazardly searching a variety of untested resources on the internet. There is an opportunity to look to systems like Japan, where teachers, subject specialists and researchers are given opportunities to collaborate through lesson study to develop high-quality instructional materials that are accessible to all.

Considering the purpose: When curriculum aims are considered meaningfully, curriculum and pedagogy cannot be thought about in isolation. The notion of pedagogical repertoires is important for understanding how different teaching approaches develop different aspects of learning. Rather than falsely polarising instructional modes against each other, they are more helpfully conceptualised for teachers in terms of their potential strengths and limitations, pitfalls and conditions for success.

Knowing (and living) our values: Values can be developed alongside and through the development of knowledge, concepts and skills. In the sustainable fashion topic mentioned in this chapter, children gained empathy for the human experiences of those affected by a highly polluting global industry in the context of their geography and English learning.

Notions of autonomy and agency: Developing children's learning autonomy through a focus on nurturing positive habits of mind, oracy and dialogue and playful enquiry are best served when embedded within teaching of the curriculum and not considered separate aims to a curriculum. Practically speaking, it is unlikely that schools have time to schedule 'learning how to learn' lessons, nor might these be desirable if separated from the actual curriculum material to grapple with and reflect on.

Curriculum design and professional development: It is a missed opportunity to separate curriculum and professional development. Teachers' literacy of curriculum materials, subject, pedagogical content and progression knowledge can be developed through a focus on curriculum development where collaborative practitioner research can facilitate planning, observing and reflecting on the efficacy of instruction. Through the core planning processes necessary in high quality teaching, teachers engage in a mode of professional learning that develops practicable knowledge for teaching.

Spaces: The physical and symbolic space of the classroom in many ways mediate the experienced curriculum. If a curriculum aims to teach the heart as well as the mind, the importance of human interactions through which children learn and reflect on knowledge might easily be underestimated when considering curriculum design. More broadly, invisible classroom norms are a powerful prism through which the intended curriculum is experienced. Children learn what to expect when they enter a school and a classroom, and this likely impacts on social and motivational aspects of learning alongside the quality of the pupil-to-pupil dialogue that takes place.

Mindful possibilities: Physical and emotional health can be marginalised within a focus on an academic curriculum. Whereas in other countries such as China, where physical exercise is strongly valued and culturally embedded, habits are much more variable in the west, as are norms around eating and nutrition. Our school has worked to give attention to these through daily class exercise, mindfulness and family-style dining routines. Similarly, therapeutic approaches to working with children are employed where appropriate and for children with trauma and attachment difficulties. It is widely documented that physical and emotional health are key components of life satisfaction in adults. It would follow then that a curriculum should pay due attention and time to developing these in daily schooling.

Towards a global curriculum: The choice of curriculum content beyond the basics of a national curriculum represent values of what issues are important for the future. Through efforts to provide a 'knowledge-rich' curriculum, there is commonly an emphasis on powerful knowledge of the past but these also need to be connected to pressing global curriculum issues of the present and future.

In light of the numerous and considerable challenges facing societies across the world, curriculums hold within them the potential of hope. Hope that future generations will act and make complex decisions in intelligent and compassionate ways. Hope that citizens can, alongside knowledge, skills and ideas for advancement, also carry with them 'ways of being' that enable them to bring about sustainable change. Because of this, pedagogy and curriculum must work in unison; how they interact during a child's education is of real significance. If we want to make claims to 'preparing our students for a world we cannot possibly imagine' (Wiliam, 2011), we need to be confident that our enacted curriculum is imbued with the types of positive relationships, values and experiences that will empower learners to release their own imaginations now and far into the future.

References

Alexander, R. (ed.) (2010) *Children, Their World, Their Education: Final Report and Recommendations of the Cambridge Primary Review*. London: Routledge.

Alexander, R. (2017) *Towards Dialogic Teaching*, 5th edition. York: Dialogos.

Autor, D.H., Levy, F. & Murnane, R.J. (2003) The skill content of recent technological change: An empirical exploration. *The Quarterly Journal of Economics*, 118(4): 1279–1333.

Biddulph, J. (2017) *The Diverse Diversities of Creative Learning at Home: Three Case Studies of Ethnic Minority Immigrant Children*, PhD Thesis. Cambridge: Cambridge University.

Biddulph, J., Rolls, L. & Smith, A. (2017) *Curriculum Design Statement*. University of Cambridge Primary School. Available online: http://universityprimarys

chool.org.uk/wp-content/uploads/2015/07/UCPS-Curriculum-Design-St atement.pdf [accessed 2 April 2019].

Bronson, M. (2000) *Self-Regulation in Early Childhood: Nature and Nurture*. New York/London: Guilford Press.

Burke, C., Barfield, J. & Peacock, A. (2016) Creating a space for irresistible learning. In: Gronn, P. & Biddulph, J. (eds) *A University's Challenge: A School for the Nation*. Cambridge: Cambridge University Press.

Burnard, P., Ross, V., Dragovic, T., Powell, K., Minors, H. & Mackinlay, E. (eds) (2017) *Building Interdisciplinary and Intercultural Bridges: Where Practice Meets Research and Theory*. Cambridge: BIBACC Publishing. ISBN 978-0-9957727-0-0.

Central Advisory Council for Education (England) (1967) *Children and Their Primary Schools: A Report of the Central Advisory Council for Education (England) (the Plowden Report)*. London: HMSO.

Coltman, P. (2006) Talk of a number: Self regulated use of mathematical metalanguage by children in the foundation stage. *Early Years*, 26(1): 31–48.

Costa, A. & Kallick, B. (2008) Habits of mind in the curriculum. In: Costa, A. & Kallick, B. (eds) *Learning and Leading with Habits of Mind: 16 Essential Characteristics for Success*. Alexandria, VA: ASCD Publications.

Educational Endowment Foundation (2015) Durham University. Available online: educationalendowmentfoundation.org.uk/public/files/Projects/ Evaluation_Reports/EEF_Project_Report_PhilosophyForChildren.pdf [accessed 10 April 2019].

Goswami, U. (2015) *Children's Cognitive Development and Learning*. York: Cambridge Primary Review Trust.

Gronn, P. & Biddulph, J. (eds) (2016) *A University's Challenge*. Cambridge: Cambridge University Press.

Hargreaves, E. and Rolls, L. (2020) *Unlocking Research: Inspiring Professional Development*. London: Routledge.

Hart, S., Drummond, M.J., Dixon, A. & McIntyre, D. (2004) *Learning Without Limits*. Maidenhead: Open University Press.

Howe, C. & Abedin, M. (2013) Classroom dialogue: A systematic review across four decades of research. *Cambridge Journal of Education*, 43(3): 325–356.

James, M., McCormick, R., Black, P., Carmichael, P., Drummond, M.J., Fox, A., MacBeath, J., Marshall, B., Pedder, D., Procter, R. & Swaffield, S. (2007) *Improving Learning: How to Learn: Classrooms, Schools and Networks*. London: Routledge.

Luckin, R., Baines, E., Cukurova, M., Holmes, W. & Mann, M. (2017) *Solved! Making the Case for Collaborative Problem-Solving*. London: NESTA.

Meyer, D. & Turner, J.C. (2002) Using instructional discourse analysis to study scaffolding of student self-regulation. *Educational Psychologist*, 37(1): 17–25.

Millard, W. & Menzies, L. (2016) Oracy: The state of speaking in our schools, London. *Voice*, 21.

O'Connor, C. & Stagnitti, K. (2011) Play, behaviour, language and social skills: The comparison of a play and a non-play intervention within a specialist School Setting. *Research in Developmental Disabilities*, 32(3): 1205–1211. doi:10.1016/j.ridd.2010.12.037.

Phillipson, N. & Wegerif, R. (2016) *Dialogic Education*. London: Routledge.

Rudduck, J. & Flutter, J. (2004) *Improving Learning Through Consulting Pupils*. Oxford: Routledge.

Schunk, D.H. & Zimmerman, B.J. (eds) (2008) *Motivation and Self-Regulated Learning: Theory, Research and Applications*. Mahwah, NJ: Lawrence Erlbaum.

Swann, M., Peacock, A., Hart, S. & Drummond, M.J. (2012) *Creating Learning Without Limits*. Maidenhead: McGraw-Hill International.

Tyrell, J. (2001) *The Power of Fantasy in Early Learning*. London: Routledge.

The Warwick Commission (2015) *Enriching Britain: Culture, Creativity and Growth. The Report of the 2015 Warwick Commission on the Future of Cultural Value*. Warwick: The University of Warwick.

Wellman, H.M. (1988) First steps in the child's theorizing about the mind. In: Astington, J., Harris, P.L. & Olson, D.R. (eds) *Developing Theories of Mind*. Cambridge: Cambridge University Press.

Whitebread, D. (ed.) (2000) *The Psychology of Teaching and Learning in the Primary School*. London: RoutledgeFalmer.

Whitebread, D. & Basilio, M. (2012) The emergence and early development of self-regulation in young children. *Profesorado: Journal of Curriculum and Teacher Education, Monograph Issue: Learn to learn. Teaching and Evaluation of self-regulated learning*, 16(1), 15–34.

Whitebread, D. & Jameson, H. (2010) Play beyond the Foundation Stage: Story-telling, creative writing and self-regulation in able 6–7 year olds. In: J. Moyles (ed.) *The Excellence of Play*, 3rd Ed. (pp. 95–107). Maidenhead: Open University Press.

Whitebread, D., Anderson, H., Coltman, P., Page, C., Pino Pasternak, D. & Mehta, S. (2005) Developing independent learning in the early years. *Education 3-13*, 33(1): 40–50.

Whitebread, D. & Coltman, P. (2016) Ensuring developmentally appropriate practice in the early years of primary schooling. In: Gronn, P. & Biddulph, J. (eds) *A University's Challenge: A School for the Nation*. Cambridge: Cambridge University Press.

Wiliam, D. (2011) How to prepare students for a world we cannot possibly imagine. *Salzburg Global Seminar*. Available online: www.dylanwiliam.org [accessed 10 April 2019].

Williams, R.D. (2008) 'Faith, reason and quality assurance - having faith in academic life', lecture given at the University of Cambridge in the series. *A World to Believe in - Cambridge Consultations on Faith, Humanity and the Future*, 21 February.

Rethinking spaces for learning
Designing a curriculum with freedom and flexibility at its heart

Kate Fox and Jonathan Clarke with support from *John-Mark Winstanley* and *Jane Warwick*

What is the purpose of primary education? What should a school be? They are questions articulated in the Cambridge Primary Review. Across the world, in every classroom, answers are attempted and more questions are formed. One answer arises in the work of Cathy Burke, Julia Barfield and Alison Peacock: "The school should be a safe, secure and nurturing environment, inwardly containing but outwardly looking and ambitious. There should be a balance struck between nurture and independence, between rigour and freedom, and between inclusion and openness" (Burke, Barfield and Peacock, 2016: p. 62).

This chapter presents a course of action to consider the environment to design a curriculum through. It presents the work of one average-sized village school in Cambridgeshire, where principled leadership and values-informed practice have transformed children's learning experiences, the physical environment, school culture and pedagogical approach. It will explore the way in which school leaders responded to their concern that provision at the school did not meet children's needs as they transitioned from flexible, child-centred early years pedagogy to more formal traditional teacher-led approaches. Written in December 2018, following the retirement of the school's long-serving headteacher, this chapter will provide a retrospective account of the school's journey over the past seven years. First, it will explore the distinctive elements of the school and identify the rationale and principles that have informed its innovative approach. Following this description, the changes made to provision will be analysed through a theoretical lens, making links to the academic literature which supports the decisions made. Finally, the chapter will detail the process of change that the school passed through in adopting its current model of teaching and learning, reflecting upon the key factors which supported the school's success.

Within this account, there is no doubt that many of the challenges and actions described will prove recognisable to those working across the primary sector.

Notwithstanding, it is the combination of spatial, curricular and interpersonal elements at play here which prove interesting – particularly the way in which they create a framework which cultivates children's ownership, independence and agency.

Strongly associated with academic and social success into adulthood, children's agency has long been championed as a foundation for children's education. In a major, large-scale study conducted by Harvard University called "The Influence of Teaching" (part of Harvard's Achievement Gap Initiative), Professor Ron Ferguson and colleagues concluded that agency plays a significant role in achievement in school: "Agency is the capacity and propensity to take purposeful initiative – the opposite of helplessness. Young people with high levels of agency do not respond passively to their circumstances; they tend to seek meaning and act with purpose to achieve the conditions they desire in their own and others' lives. The development of agency may be as important an outcome of schooling as the skills we measure with standardised testing" (Ferguson et al., 2015). The question for us was how to develop agency and independence so that there was increased ownership of the children's learning. And how would we evidence progress and high expectations?

Reasons for change: practice which limited agency

The school's innovative model for learning evolved following senior leaders' and governors' analysis of the learning habits of children and the progress they made over time. They noticed a particular issue with children in Year 1 as they transitioned from the Early Years Foundation Stage (EYFS). Through tracking these children carefully, leaders recognised that their independence, self-motivation and imagination were inhibited by the constraints of a conventional KS1 classroom. School leaders were also acutely aware that, within the confines of a class of 30, there were reduced opportunities for authentic interaction and freedom to be actively engaged and they felt that their pupils' behaviour was indicative of the need for change. In the headteacher's words: "It felt like we were trying to fit square pegs in round holes".

They were troubled that the holistic and balanced approach to teaching and learning established in EYFS had become lost as children progressed into key stages 1 and 2. Evidence suggests that this is not only an issue for this school; Fisher (2008) presents considerable research evidence which indicates that, as children progress through education, they become increasingly disillusioned and disaffected. She concluded that formal education "can inhibit some of the prominent characteristics of competent young learners" (p. 1). The reasons for this are attributed to an increasingly prescriptive education system which has been dominated by a performativity culture over the last 30 years, leading many teachers to adopt a reductive pedagogy which restricts children's ownership over their own learning.

A tour of the school

Entering into the Foundation Stage, you observe the things you would expect: children engrossed in the outdoor role-play area; practitioners sitting on the floor skilfully questioning their guided groups; a group of children happily creating junk-models, completely immersed in their creations. Practice here exemplifies the principles of the Development Matters Framework in the Early Years Foundation Stage (DfE, 2012):

- Every child is a unique child who is constantly learning and can be resilient, capable, confident and self-assured.
- Children learn to be strong and independent through positive relationships.
- Children learn and develop well in enabling environments, in which their experiences respond to their individual needs and there is a strong partnership between practitioners and parents and carers.
- Children develop and learn in different ways … . Practitioners teach children by ensuring challenging, playful opportunities across the prime and specific areas of learning and development.

It is only when you move around the school that you become aware that many of the pedagogical principles seen within EYFS have been implemented into Key Stages 1 and 2. By doing this, the school subscribes to Whitebread's (2012) argument that children do not simply learn what they are taught, but what they experience. This highlights the importance of teachers who consider not only the learning activity, but also the entire classroom environment and ethos which inspires children to be active in their learning (Figure 4.1).

Stepping outdoors, you discover a group of Year 1 and 2 children in the outdoor classroom, working with a specialist Teaching Assistant (TA) to develop their knowledge of food chains. The utilisation of outdoor environments for learning is an important part of life at the school and all children in Key Stage 1 spend at least one session a week in this classroom and in other outdoor spaces.

Meanwhile, a determined Year 1 boy stands proudly on the outdoor covered decking, skilfully negotiating the challenge of painting on an easel on a windy day, surrounded by the laughter and joy of another group of children exploring the role-play area. A few steps inside, you find yourself amongst equally captivated children: some using oil pastels to recreate the peacock feathers displayed in front of them, others crafting junk models of a 3D bird. Each group is guided by an expert practitioner, intervening when appropriate and asking questions which challenge each child's thinking. Stepping through a doorway, the exciting buzz of collaborative learning is counterpointed by the gentle sound of classical music. Sitting peacefully at a horseshoe table, a group of children are immersed

Figure 4.1 Brightly coloured walls with one of the school's mottos painted above the Independent Learning Zone area in Year 3/4

in writing a non-chronological report about barn owls whilst their teacher circulates and provides each child with feedback. The quality of verbal and written work produced by 5–6-year olds is striking; they speak so confidently about what they have learnt, incorporating an impressive use of technical vocabulary (Figure 4.2).

Moving into Key Stage 2, you could be forgiven for thinking you were entering the head office of a media company: children sit on sofas completing their artwork; others perch along a bench in front of a bank of computer workstations creating adverts, whilst another group of children and a TA collaboratively solve maths problems, jotting their calculations directly onto a whiteboard table. Amid this hubbub of activity, one boy is transported into another world as he reads silently on a sofa. Through a decorated archway, the teachers are leading groups of children through their guided group work. One small group is engaged in a fruitful discussion about adverbial clauses whilst the other tackles complex mathematical word problems (Figure 4.3).

Several things strike you as you spend time in this atypical learning space:

- impressive open physical environment
- outdoor learning spaces constantly used for children to learn in

Figure 4.2 The Independent Learning Zone area in Year 5/6 with banks of computers for children to undertake their own research. Sofas and other soft furniture are provided so children can choose where they would like to work

- high levels of children's agency and independence
- motivated and articulate learners throughout the school
- on-task behaviour and industrious work ethic from learners of all ages
- highly skilled, confident adults
- dialogic approach (Littleton & Mercer, 2013) of all adults
- community of learning for all
- everyone in the school is engaged in a collective and collaborative endeavour of learning.

Figure 4.3 The Year 5/6 classroom – small groups work at the two central tables with the teacher while others work at the small tables or sit on the sofas to complete independent work

Hemingford Grey Primary School is a welcoming, caring school in which pupils develop the skills and the security that they need to become enquiring and confident learners. Staff and pupils have worked, together, to define the school's values of "resourcefulness, reflectiveness, resilience, relationships, risk-taking and respect". These are a lived reality in the school's day-to-day life and work. Pupils are unfailingly polite and cooperative in their learning and during social times. They get to work quickly, are keen to find out new things, and know how to do so. They keep trying when they encounter difficulty. Pupils enjoy thinking deeply about the "big questions" that they are asked to consider. They listen carefully to each other's views and understand, in the words of one pupil, that "sometimes getting it wrong first helps you to get it right later".

(Ofsted, June 2018)

How does it work?

The school has four Learning Zones:

- Foundation Stage (with 45 children)
- Key Stage 1 (three mixed Year 1/2 classes)
- Lower Key Stage 2 (three mixed Year 3/4 classes)
- Upper Key Stage 2 (three mixed Year 5/6 classes).

In a bid to promote authentic opportunities for independence, and to allow children to take ownership of their learning, the school knocked down the walls (both physical and metaphorical) between classrooms to create these dynamic spaces for learning. In doing this, the school wanted to further reduce any barriers – in this case the physical environment which restricted children's free-flow – limiting the autonomy and creativity of its pupils and staff. This bold choice links to research surrounding the Reggio Emilia approach which identifies three key stakeholders in a child's education: parent, teacher and the environment. By restructuring the learning environment in this way, the school was able to explore the myriad of ways that space can be utilised to "speak" to children and empower them as learners (Fraser, 2006).

Within each Zone, children are taught English and Mathematics (referred to as the Basic Skills within the school) by their teachers in groups of up to 15 children. Groups are fluid, can be sub-grouped and are organised according to the changing needs of the cohort. When they are not involved in a teacher focus group, children are engaged in a range of structured independent and collaborative learning opportunities facilitated by teachers and led by highly skilled and well-trained teaching assistants. Here, children are expected to complete a number of tasks which require them to practise and apply skills from across the National Curriculum. Often, the order in which children complete these tasks and the way in which they produce their work is left up to them. They benefit from a huge amount of trust and, thanks to the hard work that staff have put into developing their independence and high-calibre learning attitudes, they produce work of high quality.

The curriculum

The school has developed a curriculum which they hope will spark intrigue and motivation. The humanities and children's development as global citizens are threaded through every theme of the curriculum, which was designed primarily with the needs of the school's children in mind. Each theme begins with a broad question which links past, current and future thinking, and children's knowledge and skills are developed through cross-curricular learning which enables them to answer this question at a deep level. In KS2, the theme question is broken down into fortnightly 'Big Questions' which enable the children to develop as independent researchers and to formulate opinions about the information they gather. Investment in a strong resource base for all aspects of learning makes this possible. The impact of the approach to the curriculum is that children's learning is not purely knowledge driven but enables the pupils to apply their learning to the issues of today so that they are able to develop well-informed opinions. The benefits of this were evidenced in the school's most recent Ofsted report:

> You have focused upon ensuring that from the time that they join the school, all pupils learn how to plan pieces of work, complete research, and use different ways to solve problems or to present their findings or ideas. By the time pupils reach key stage 2, these ways of working become second nature. They help pupils to find things out for themselves, to show resilience in the face of difficulty, and to evaluate information and ideas. Pupils also learn how to use knowledge and skills in one subject to enhance their learning in another.
>
> *(Ofsted, June 2018)*

As an alternative to a prescriptive and rigid curriculum, which poses the danger of disempowering children and their potential to learn (Fisher, 2008), the school aims to provide a broad and creative curriculum in which children can actively choose the direction of the learning outcome. A visit to the school demonstrates that children are excited to engage in enquiry-based learning and explore potential answers to the big questions they have been set.

Maximising learning capacity

The school's collaborative, industrious and innovative approach embodies many of the principles championed within Hart, Dixon, Drummond and McIntyre's (2004) "Learning without Limits", which explored ways of teaching designed to maximise the learning capacity of all children. When describing a school's ability to provide transformative learning experiences, Hart et. al (2004) stated that:

> This will come about through the work of the teacher: by continually extending and enhancing learning opportunities, reducing and removing existing limits, progressively transforming the states of mind that condition young people's choices about whether to engage and how much to invest in the learning opportunities provided for them in school.
>
> *(p. 170)*

It could be argued that it is the framework created at the school, comprising the curriculum the school provides, the environment it creates and the classroom relationships it fosters, which allows teachers to achieve this. For example, and as previously noted, children working in the school's Learning Zones are often invited to work independently and are regularly given the choice about how they will produce evidence of their learning. By providing the children with such choices, the school is subverting the asymmetrical power balance which pervades many classrooms and is establishing a culture of co-agency which is championed within Learning without Limits (2004):

> What teachers must try to do, in all their classroom decision-making and in every teaching and learning encounter, is to use their own power (over the external forces that enable and constrain learning capacity) to affect how young people choose to use their power.
>
> *(p. 180)*

Hart et. al (2004) argue that, through providing the children with increased agency in their learning, a school can motivate its young learners to become active participants in the teaching and learning process:

> Such open tasks and opportunities for choice reflect the principle of co-agency, because part of their intention is not just to facilitate access and engagement but to reinforce young people's active sense of their powers and competence as thinkers and learners, that what they have to bring and contribute to their own learning is important, valued and welcomed in the classroom.
>
> *(p. 185)*

The way in which the school achieves this is captured through the words of Jack, aged 8, who states that:

> We love being able to choose what we do in the Learning Zones. It's nice to be able to do things on your own, like how you want to do it, because you enjoy it more and you learn so much more better.

Habits of mind: learning to learn

Clearly structured behaviour management approaches have a place in every school, and at Hemingford Grey Primary School these were developed alongside the children's school council. Alongside this, inspired by the work of Dweck (2012) and Claxton (2002), the school has placed a strong emphasis on developing positive habits of mind and a clear learning orientation in children. This can be seen from the school's values, represented in Figure 4.4. In turn, focus is placed on creating a culture which values hard work and champions learning as a difficult process. Children talk openly about the complexities of learning and can articulate a positive attitude surrounding the importance of making mistakes. This is because when children enter the school in the Foundation Stage, they learn about the qualities and attitudes needed to enable them to approach the challenges of learning positively, with determination to succeed. Long-term plans have been adapted to incorporate aspects of Dweck's (2012) Mindset work and Claxton's (2002) Building Learning Power so that children are regularly reminded and taught about the habits of mind needed to be a successful learner. This has resulted in a culture where every member of the community is expected to be a learner, that mistakes can be learned from and that effort is the key factor which can influence improvement. As one child in Year 5 eloquently puts it:

> Learning is great because we learn from mistakes and come across confusing things but understand that climbing out of the pit is extraordinary because you have the feeling you are brilliant and can do everything.

This quote is representative of the way in which the school's approach has allowed them to develop a "pedagogy of self-regulation", described by Whitebread (2012) as dependent upon four underlying principles (Figure 4.4):

- emotional warmth and security
- feelings of control
- cognitive challenge
- articulation of learning.

Figure 4.4 The school's values based on the work of Dweck and Claxton

The power of relationships

Perhaps another reason why children are excited to learn is due to the quality of relationships evident throughout the school. This has been facilitated by the way in which the school approaches teaching and learning: all children work regularly with adults and, in the words of the headteacher: "No one falls under the radar".

By organising children into flexible groups, who either work with their teacher or undertake independent activities within the Learning Zones at different points in the day, the school has worked creatively to address the challenges associated with managing classes of up to 30 children. Teachers and teaching assistants work with groups and individuals much more effectively as a result. Whilst the school is aware of recent studies which claim that reducing class sizes may have a very limited impact on pupil outcomes, they champion the fundamental importance of 'interthinking' (Littleton & Mercer, 2013) between teachers and pupils and are confident that their approach provides them with the capacity to engage meaningfully with each of their pupils as individual learners.

The school is proud that every child benefits from high-quality input within a small group, where teaching can be contingently tailored to their specific needs. Working with these small groups, teachers and teaching assistants can tune into the progress of all children during lessons and thus swiftly intervene through providing immediate feedback which moves their learning forward. Supported by a plethora of research which exhorts the high impact of regular feedback (i.e. Black & Wiliam, 1998), school leaders believe that it is the dialogue facilitated by these small group interactions that ensures their success as it provides regular opportunities for teachers and pupils to engage in conversations about progress. Moreover, it also provides teachers and pupils with regular opportunities to get to learn about each other, thus forming more positive relationships on a deeper level and resulting in an increased commitment to the shared endeavour of teaching and learning. Wood (2017) argues that it is the power of such relationships that can increase pupils' belief in their own competence, leading to increased motivation, autonomy and academic success. Drawing upon evidence which advocates the combined benefit of positive teacher-pupil relationships and regular feedback, it is suggested that pupils are more likely to engage with their learning and make more progress if they feel valued by the teachers they work with. This is something which can be identified easily when visiting the school and is a factor which has high value amongst the school community, as articulated in the following comment from the school's Deputy Head:

> Relationships are what Hemingford Grey is all about and are the reason why I have stayed at the school for so long. The way we do things means that you have the time to talk to children and understand them as learners much more deeply. My teaching is so much stronger as a result – I feel I really understand

what the children need, can talk to them more openly about how they can move their learning forward and that they are so much more informed as learners who feel valued and recognised as individuals.

Inclusive learning environment

Key to the school's success in forming positive relationships has been its ability to avoid practice which undermines its belief in equal opportunities for all. School leaders possess an unceasing commitment to creating an inclusive ethos where all children are individually valued and cared for and where all staff are expected to work hard to remove barriers to learning and success. Making this vision a reality has required a significant shift in school mindset to create an authentic inclusive learning environment where children and adults are expected to take risks. This is based on a thoughtful, active and positive view of children as individuals who can support and extend their own learning (Kershner, 2009). Through the revised physical structure of the school's learning zones and the subsequent focus on groups and individuals, the school promotes pupils' dialogue, collaboration, choice and explorations and also establishes an environment in which it is assumed that all pupils are capable of learning (Kershner, 2009). Because every child is taught in a mixture of small group, paired or individual scenarios, within an open space, the need to withdraw any child to carry out a particular intervention is eradicated. As a result, children identified as having special educational needs avoid any sense of stigma associated with the support they receive or from being withdrawn, as all children benefit from a similar experience. Consequently, distribution of resources – particularly teacher and TA time – is far more equitable and responsive to children's changing needs. Moreover, the flexibility of the school's groupings means that there is no need to assign traditional labels associated with ability. This empowers the children even further as it removes any limitations or assumptions that could restrict their progress as individuals, yet again drawing parallels with the Learning without Limits project (2004).

The physical environment

In order for the principles of The Foundation Stage curriculum (EYFS) to become implemented and embedded throughout Key Stages 1 and 2, the physical environment needed to be changed which, as a result, has become a striking feature. The Leadership Team worked with the builders to design and construct a more flexible space with breakout areas, large open corridors and ease of movement between the different zones. In doing this, they were keen to establish spaces for play, challenge, enquiry, reflection, dialogue and collaboration so that the environment would facilitate "the extensive variety of ways in which a child might be engaged in school life", striking a balance between the need to respect individuality and community. Through such changes, the school environment was transformed into a "non-hierarchical and highly democratic space" where learning was made possible in all areas (Burke, Barfield and Peacock, 2016, p. 62). This enables the staff to work with different groups of children in different areas and moves away from the traditional 'classroom box'. This draws parallels with research carried out by Hertzberger (2008), who promoted the concept of an 'articulated classroom' which "provides more spaces for different groups or individuals to engage in different activities simultaneously in a room without being unduly distracted by each other. So the number of options are greater here, there being several centres of attention rather than just the one" (p. 24).

The walls are generally painted in a light colour with at least one wall being painted in a bright colour and motivational quotes written up across the spaces to create a light, airy and modern space as seen in Figures 4.1–4.3. Many of the newly created conditions evident in the school have been highlighted in a recent study which revealed a 16% impact of school design on children's academic performance in reading, writing and maths. The three year 'Holistic Evidence and Design' (HEAD) study of 153 classrooms in 27 English primary schools by Barrett, Davies, Zhang and Barrett (2017) found that all three parameters on the 'Individualisation' theme; 'ownership', 'flexibility' and 'connection' significantly positively correlated with increases in pupil outcomes. These conditions and pedagogy were consistent throughout the school. Barrett et al. report that architectural design elements account for roughly 25% of the impact on learning.

> A classroom that has distinct architectural characteristics, e.g. unique location (bungalow, or separate buildings); shape (L shape; T shape); ... facilities specially-designed for pupils, ... also seems to strengthen the pupils' sense of ownership.

Details about the findings from the HEAD report (Barrett et al, 2017) in relation to the 'Individualisation' theme can be found in Table 4.1 in addition to aspects from the 'stimulation' theme which were also relevant to the school – complexity and colour.

Managing change

The school's journey towards this approach required a combination of strategic thinking, attention to detail and prudent financial management. Moreover, the school took time to monitor carefully and reflect upon the effectiveness of this approach in Key Stage 1 before planning for and establishing Learning Zones in Key Stage 2. They also worked in partnership with another school, Huntingdon Primary, who were interested in developing similar provision within their own setting. This meant that the school community benefited from an alternative perspective which, although set in a contrasting context, offered a critical friendship to support the school's evolution.

Table 4.1 The main classroom characteristics that support the improvement of pupils' learning identified in the study (Barrett et al, 2017)

Design parameters	Findings from Barrett's study	Good Classroom Features for Teachers
Ownership (Distinct design feature)	Architectural design elements that make the room unique and child-centred are significantly correlated with the learning process	Classroom that has distinct design characteristic; personalised display and high-quality chairs and desks are more likely to provide a sense of ownership.
Ownership (Nature of the display)	Personal displays by the children create a 'sense of ownership' and this was significantly correlated with the learning process	Larger, simpler areas for older children, but more varied plan shapes for younger pupils.
Ownership (Furniture)	Furniture and features in the class that were ergonomic and comfortable for the children were significantly correlated with learning process	Easy access to attached breakout space and widened corridor for pupils' storage. Well-defined learning zones that facilitate age-appropriate learning options, plus a big wall area for display.
Flexibility (Room layout)	Flexibility measures investigated in this study were breakout spaces and rooms, storage solutions, number of different learning zones and potential display area. More learning zones for younger children correlated with learning progress. Breakout zones within the room were correlated with learning progress.	Well-defined and age appropriate learning zones are important to facilitate learning. Younger pupils need several well-defined zones for play-based learning activities. For older pupils, simpler space configurations support more formal teaching.
Flexibility (Size)	Larger rooms with simpler shapes (squarer) enabled older children to better function in whole class learning. However, complex room shapes for younger children facilitated learning zones and enabled flexibility.	Lower height furniture provides more wall area available for varied displays.
Stimulation (Complexity)	The room layout, ceiling and display can catch the pupils' attention but in balance with a degree of order without cluttered and noisy feelings.	The room layout, ceiling and display can catch the pupils' attention but in balance with a degree of order without cluttered and noisy feelings.
Stimulation (Colour)	White walls with a feature wall (highlighting with vivid and or light colour) produces a good level of stimulation. Bright colour on furniture and display are introduced as accents to the overall environment.	White walls with a feature wall (highlighting with vivid and or light colour) produces a good level of stimulation. Bright colour on furniture and display are introduced as accents to the overall environment.

Leading the school through this period of change was by no means an easy feat and school leaders speak openly about the hard work and resilience staff have had to show to make the Learning Zones a success. Interestingly, many of the factors school leaders have identified as key to their success draw parallels with Holmes, Clement and Albright's (2013) literature review exploring the complex task of leading change in schools. For example, school leaders articulated that their main priority was to ensure that a shared vision, built upon a clear moral purpose, was established through collaboration with all stakeholders. Secondly, school leaders were keen that they established a culture of trust, whilst also developing individual staff so that they possessed the skills needed to flourish within the school's new approach. By placing such a focus on supporting school staff throughout this period of change, school leaders showed an awareness of Fullan and Hargreaves' (1991) argument that:

> However noble, sophisticated, or enlightened proposals for change and improvement might be, they come to nothing if teachers do not adopt them in their own classrooms and if they do not translate them into effective classroom practice.
>
> *(p. 13)*

Historically, high quality, appropriate professional development (PD) is something that the school has always been committed to, and invested heavily in, providing opportunities for staff to translate vision into their daily practice. In the case of introducing the Learning Zones, school leaders initially organised for all teachers and teaching assistants to visit Middlefield Primary Academy (Cambridgeshire) and West Thornton Academy (Croydon) where a similar philosophy and practice was already established. Immersing staff in the practice at both schools enabled them to reach a shared understanding of what Hemingford Grey Primary School could look like. Following this, a strategic PD plan was developed which would support staff to understand the significant shift in school culture and pedagogical content knowledge that the school's new approach would demand. This drew upon expertise both within and outside of the school and, once again, was based on school leaders' understanding that effective change was dependent upon effective staff development. As Fullan (1986) argues:

> Changes in teaching practices and in underlying beliefs are to do with changes in doing and thinking respectively. It is not easy for people, even if willing, to change their behaviour and thinking significantly. Yet this is exactly what is at stake in implementing educational changes. Incidentally, it is for this reason that effective professional development goes hand in hand with effective implementation.
>
> *(p. 322)*

Developing trust and equipping parents and carers to understand and support the school's vision

In addition to measures put in place through formal training, school leaders worked hard to establish the culture of trust which they viewed as essential. This is a belief shared by Kochanek (2005) who, drawing upon research surrounding trust in schools, identifies a positive relationship between trust and school effectiveness; makes a connection between the growth of trust and organisational changes and suggests that this ultimately leads to improved educational outcomes for students. Leaders recognised that they were embarking on a journey which would involve moving significantly away from conventional models for learning. With this in mind, they saw that there had to be a different approach to the hierarchical monitoring which had been commonplace, particularly in relation to classroom observations. They feared that observations that had traditionally been carried out solely by senior leaders risked creating the perception that teachers were being judged, rather than being supported, to align their practice to this new model. Therefore, it was decided that all teachers and teaching assistants would be routinely invited to observe each other's practice alongside school leaders. As part of this, teachers and teaching assistants were expected to provide constructive and developmental feedback to their peers, supported by members of the leadership team. This subverted the power relationship traditionally associated with lesson observations and shifted the focus of feedback from criticism to collective problem solving. In addition to increasing opportunities for collaboration, this decision also provided further opportunities for professional development wherein all staff could reflect upon and evaluate the quality of provision across the school. This openness of practice ensures a high level of confidence in the quality of the input and support that all children receive from all staff in each Zone. In addition, it means that all staff are inspired to operate at the highest level and to learn from each other, irrespective of age, stage or position. Through this approach, leaders have real confidence that the vision is a lived reality.

In addition to establishing trust amongst staff, school leaders were also aware of the need to extend this culture to the wider school community, particularly parents. Accordingly, the school offered a range of opportunities for parents and carers to celebrate their children's learning and to see first-hand how the Learning Zone model operated on a day-to-day basis. Additionally, trust was further developed by supporting parents and carers to develop their own skills and subject knowledge through a range of workshops in key areas led by school staff with particular skills and knowledge. Parents and carers also had the opportunity to drop in for coffee with the Headteacher, Deputy Headteacher and a representative from the Governing Body to share their views, offer ideas and receive informal updates about school development. The school's genuine open-door policy allows parents and carers to learn more about the Learning Zones, as well as ask questions and raise any issues they may have. Leaders gathered feedback from parents which told them that these opportunities were highly valued and supportive in helping them to help their children and understand the way the school operated.

Conclusion

Overall, there is much to learn from this school. It provides us with an example of a setting which had the courage to change its curriculum, pedagogy and environment to match the team's unwavering values and beliefs in the potential of children to work independently to produce work of a very high quality. The school's key strength lies in its refusal to 'rest on its laurels' and to continuously seek out ways to improve outcomes for the community it serves, not only in terms of testing outcomes but also attitudes, levels of motivation and engagement, independent skills and habits of mind. A significant point to note is that, prior to implementing the Learning Zone model, the school was not in *need* of change – standards were consistently 'good' and the school community expressed high levels of satisfaction in the school's work. Notwithstanding, the school applied a critical lens to its daily work and, after realising that there could be an even more effective way of educating its children, took the brave decision to take a risk and embrace change.

Within an increasingly prescriptive system, where the demands of performativity often force schools into adopting compliant models of teaching and learning, Hemingford Grey's willingness to take a risk should not be underestimated. By doing this, the school itself had to draw upon its core values of resourcefulness, reflectiveness, resilience, relationships, risk-taking and respect and, in turn, has provided the children with a model which will inspire them and equip them with the skills to do this for themselves. Moreover, an important note to reflect upon is that the school provides a model of how to negotiate the challenges of accountability, reconceptualising the notion of "vertical accountability" which aims to meet the demands of government policy, to a "horizontal accountability" which places the needs of its community at the heart of all its endeavours above all else (Barzano & Brotto, 2009).

Other key messages which stand out are:

- the power of trust
- the importance of collaborative enterprise
- the significance of high-quality professional learning to manage change effectively.

Significantly, this chapter serves as a call to action for all stakeholders in the education system to dare to be different – not just for the sake of it – but to provide children with the very best learning experience possible not for just today but for their future lives.

Reflective task 1

Take a walk around your own school – what strikes you about the learning environment? The children's learning behaviours? The culture? The relationship between learners and adults?

Does the school provide what you believe the children need?

Reflective task 2

What are the central principles, values and aims of your curriculum? Can all members of the school community articulate these? How do you bring these to life?

Reflective task 3

How do the children at your school understand the concept of learning as a process?

How are the children explicitly taught about how to be an effective learner?

Do children – and adults – understand that mistakes are a fundamental aspect of the learning process?

Reflective task 4

What is the quality of relationships like within your setting?

Between children and staff?

Between staff?

Between the school and the wider community?

What time is provided to invest in these relationships?

Reflective task 5

How many of the features identified in Table 4.1 are evident in your school?

How does the physical environment in your school enable or disable learning? What could be done to address this?

Within the constraints of your budget, what changes could be made to improve the environment? In the short term? Longer term?

Does the physical environment embody the values and principles of the school? If there is a mis-match, what could be done?

Reflective task 6

How do you support all staff to realise the vision?

How strategic is your Professional Development plan?

Is there a long-term view of the professional learning for all staff including support staff?

What do you want staff to have achieved within three years? Five years?

References

Barrett, P., Davies, F., Zhang, Y. and Barrett, L. (2017). The holistic impact of classroom spaces on learning in specific subjects. *Environment and Behavior*, 49(4), 425–451.

Barzano, G. and Brotto, F. (2009). Leadership, learning and Italy: A tale of atmospheres. In: J. MacBeath and Y. C. Cheng (eds), *Leadership for Learning: International Perspectives* (pp. 223–240). Rotterdam: Sense Publishers.

Black, P. and Wiliam, D. (1998). *Inside the Black Box: Raising Standards Through Classroom Assessment*. London: Kings College.

Burke, C., Barfield, J. and Peacock, A. (2016). Creating a space for irresistable learning. In: P. Gronn and J. Biddulph (eds), *A University's Challenge Cambridge's Primary School for the Nation* (pp. 59–79). Cambridge: Cambridge University Press.

Claxton, G.L. (2002). *Building Learning Power: Helping Young People Become Better Learners*. Bristol: TLO Ltd.

Department for Education (2012) *Development Matters in the Early Years Foundation Stage*. London: Department for Education.

Dweck, C. (2012). *Mindset*. London: Robinson.

Ferguson, R., Phillips, S.F., Rowley, J.F.S. and Friedlander, J.W. (2015). The influence of teaching beyond standardized test scores: Engagement, mindsets, and agency. Harvard University. Accessed via: http://www.agi.harvard.edu/projects/TeachingandAgency.pdf.

Fisher, J. (2008). *Starting from the Child, Teaching and Learning in the Foundation Stage*. 3rd ed. Maidenhead: Open University Press.

Fraser, S. (2006). *Authentic Childhood: Experiencing Reggio Emilia in the Classroom. Albany, NY*. Nelson: Thomas Learning.

Fullan, M. (1986). Improving the implementation of educational change. *School Organization*, 6(3), 321–326.

Fullan, M. and Hargreaves, A. (1991). *What's Worth Fighting for in Your School?* Toronto: Ontario Public School Teachers' Federation; Andover, MA: The Network. Buckingham, UK: Open University Press; Melbourne: Australian Council of Educational Administration.

Hart, S., Dixon, A., Drummond, M.J. and McIntyre, D. (2004). *Learning Without Limits*. Maidenhead: Open University Press.

Hertzberger, H. (2008) *The Classroom Dethroned. In H. Hertzberger, Spaces in Learning: Lessons in Architecture 3*. [Translated John Kirkpatrick] Rotterdam: 010 Publishers.

Holmes, K., Clement, J. and Albright, J. (2013). The complex task of leading educational change in schools. *School Leadership and Management*, 33(3), 270–283.

Kershner, R. (2009). Learning in inclusive classrooms. In: P. Hick, R. Kershner and P. Farrell (eds), *Psychology for Inclusive Education: New Directions in Theory and Practice*. Abingdon: Routledge.

Konachek, J.R. (2005). *Building Trust for Better Schools: Research-Based Practices*. Thousand Oaks: SAGE.

Littleton, K. and Mercer, N. (2013). *Interthinking Putting Talk to Work*. Abingdon: Routledge.

Ofsted (2018) *Hemingford Grey Primary School Short Inspection Report*. https://files.ofsted.gov.uk/v1/file/2783165 [accessed 01/04/2020]

Whitebread, D.J. (2012). *Developmental Psychology and Early Childhood Education*. London: SAGE.

Wood, R. (2017). *The Influence of Teacher-Student Relationships and Feedback on Students' Engagement with Learning*. Newcastle upon Tyne: Cambridge Scholars Publishing.

5

"Why do I have to sit down?"

Designing an age-appropriate curriculum for children in Year 1

Rachel Sutton, Lucy Downham and Harriet Rhodes

Currently in English schools there is a disjunction between the play-based educational provision in the National Curriculum Early Years Foundation Stage (which covers the period of nursery through to the end of the reception year) and the more formal practice in the National Curriculum Key Stage 1, which steers teaching and learning in Year 1 classrooms through to the end of Year 2 (Fisher, 2009). Concern about the possible impact of this transition on children has led researchers to give specific attention to what is happening at this stage; for example, children in reception classes, interviewed for the Cambridge Primary Review team's Soundings, were worried about the loss of play and increased workload when they moved into Year 1. One child memorably described sitting on the carpet as 'wasting your life' (Alexander, 2010: 370). It is important to remember that most children may already have experienced a transitional step less than a year previously when moving from a nursery or pre-school setting into the reception class in a primary school. Many will therefore have undertaken two transitions by the time they are five-years-old. The constant adaptation to new and varied learning environments can have an impact on children's wellbeing and, as research shows, it is vitally important to meet children's emotional and social needs throughout these early stages of their lives (Brooker, 2008; Trodd, 2013; Whitebread, 2015).

This chapter follows two teachers in a Fenland school as they sought to enhance their pupils' joyful engagement with learning and their skills for self-regulated learning. The teachers noticed that their pupils appeared to be less motivated by a Year 1 curriculum which was more formal than the one they had previously experienced in the Early Years Foundation Stage: an observation which mirrors findings of wider research (Alexander, 2010). Through implementing a curriculum which celebrates children's natural inclinations for play-based learning, the teachers saw development in the children's levels of language and communication and an improvement in their learning dispositions. The teachers reflected continuously on their practice in their quest to meet the needs of their young learners, considering many aspects of their practice including the impact of the learning environment. Their overarching desire to create independent, motivated learners fuelled examination of other areas, including the creation of a skills-based curriculum, as they explored ways to promote children's agency and self-regulation. This account describes the impact these approaches made on the pupils and their teachers.

About Peckover School

Peckover School is a two-form entry primary school (part of the Brooke Weston Trust) in Wisbech, Cambridgeshire. This Fenland town is part of the East Cambridgeshire and Fenland Opportunity Area which receives additional funding and support from the government in a bid to improve social mobility within the region. Just over a quarter of the school's pupils qualify for Pupil Premium funding and 50 per cent have English as an additional language (EAL).

After achieving her degree in primary education, Rachel Sutton taught for six years, becoming Early Years Lead and Science Coordinator for the whole school. Working with Lucy Downham, who was in her Newly Qualified Teacher (NQT) year at the time, they initiated their new, play-based curriculum through a process of continual reflection and adjustment. They adapted their pedagogical approaches and classroom provision based on research evidence and on their own professional knowledge of how children learn.

Our journey into continuous provision in Year 1: Lucy and Rachel's story

In September 2016, our school had a Year 1 cohort which had high levels of need, particularly in communication, language and behaviour. Even though these children had made expected progress in the Foundation Stage, we found that their learning was slowing significantly in Year 1 and, after a term and a half, we realised that we needed to alter our practice if they were to make good progress. We knew research evidence has reported that some children, particularly those who are summer-born or who have special educational needs (SEN), were more likely to struggle in the move to a more formal learning environment (Alexander, 2010).

We believed that the more formal Year 1 teaching approach was inhibiting the children's independence, curiosity and passion to learn. We also suspected that the classroom environment was insufficiently stimulating and the amount of time children spent sitting at desks was impacting negatively on learning outcomes. They showed a lack of engagement with their learning and high levels of passivity. We were aware of psychological research which has shown that self-regulation is fundamental to the development of children's confidence and resilience (Whitebread, 2012). Although this was going to be a daunting change to our pedagogy, it was clear that we needed to adjust our practice so that the needs of the children would be met more effectively.

We decided to trial the use of continuous provision in the summer term of 2017. We defined this as giving children the opportunity for self-directed learning in play-based contexts. Children were able to choose where they wanted to learn and were encouraged to select from the range of activities offered to them. Firstly, we added more 'learning zones' and provided open-ended resources to entice children to investigate different themes. We hoped that they would show higher levels of involvement with the resources and become more absorbed in learning. However, this proved to be a disaster. In only two terms of formal learning, the children had seemingly lost their ability to be independent and were 'switched off'; they seemed to have forgotten how to play. A visitor to our classroom would have been greeted with a chaotic, disruptive class who were unable to focus on their learning in a meaningful way. We realised that the children needed assistance to generate positive play themes and to work collaboratively with their peers (Singer, Golinkoff & Hirsh-Pasek, 2006). So it was time for another re-think.

Much of the way in which we educate young children in England has been based upon the work of Russian psychologist Lev Vygotsky, whose theory of social constructivism underpins how we teach (see Vygotsky, translated 1978). He believed that learning is based on social interactions and that if children are supported or 'scaffolded' by an adult or more experienced peer, they will make greater progress. Learning is dependent on communication and interaction between the child and the more knowledgeable 'other'. We realised that our children needed to be scaffolded into learning through play-based means and in order to help them, we planned a carousel of activities which they could choose from. Some of the activities offered were adult-supported and some were accessed by the children autonomously. All activities were planned in accordance with our skills curriculum (see Tables 5.1 and 5.2). To some extent, this proved to be more successful: children were able to focus on their learning for more extensive periods and they demonstrated deeper levels of engagement. Yet this was still not how we wanted to teach as we felt that we were still restricting the children and we wanted to give them greater freedom of choice.

We then provided specific learning zones for maths, phonics and writing, which we believed would give the children purposeful, engaging learning opportunities. These proved to be unsuccessful as many children avoided these areas altogether, preferring to play with more open-ended resources which would allow them to explore their own ideas. We felt that these zones may have been too 'directed': after all, what five-year-old child would willingly pick up a maths task, select their resources and answer the questions, when they could be in the construction area building a car track with their friends and measuring how far their car would travel down the ramp? Clearly, this was how they wanted to learn. The task for us was to work out how we could facilitate this.

Towards independent learning

In Autumn 2017, with support from the Early Years and Year 2 team, we started to make changes to the physical learning environment in our classrooms. We attended conferences and training and sought advice from Early Years author Anna Ephgrave (2017) and other advisors on how to provide an enabling environment in which children would feel safe and empowered to develop their own learning ideas. The training confirmed that previously we had not been providing the children with enough open-ended opportunities and consequently this had effectively been limiting children's learning. We were hindering their ability to be curious and passionate learners by setting prescribed expectations of outcomes.

The learning space and its impact on motivation

In place of the specific learning areas (mathematics, writing and phonics), we provided areas which would encourage a greater range of learning opportunities; for example, the woodwork and construction areas could be used more effectively to promote mathematical thinking through encouraging children to investigate measures and shape. Equally, the 'small-world' area could be used to stimulate children to write the story they had just enacted. In this way we were giving ownership to the children as they were able to choose how they interacted with the resources and were consequently more highly motivated. Their levels of engagement increased because they were finding purpose in their learning (Figure 5.1).

The feeling of empowerment is a key element in enabling children to develop positive attitudes to themselves as learners. Research surrounding Attribution Theory examines how children attribute their successes and failures. If children feel that they have power over the outcome of their endeavours they will respond positively to failure; if, however, they feel powerless they will respond negatively and develop 'learned helplessness'. This destructive stance will, of course, impact on their motivation and self-esteem (Whitebread, 2008) (Figure 5.2).

Figure 5.1 Children use their mathematical skills in all areas. Here children have chosen some maths resources and paper to solve their own halving problems

Figure 5.2 This child has used a book to look at patterns. She has then created her own and written about it

Designing a whole-school curriculum

Alongside our own evaluation of provision in Year 1, the whole school was also considering how to streamline the curriculum to accommodate more immersive learning experiences and allow teachers to have greater flexibility in planning. The school collectively decided to focus on skills, believing that these are transferable and give children tools for lifelong learning. We designed a skills–based curriculum which we developed over six staff meetings (Table 5.1 shows an example of the geography curriculum). The whole staff became involved in the construction of the framework. During these meetings, we had conversations about the skills we already taught before considering those we might focus on specifically. Through this process teachers had complete ownership and understood the continuous development from Reception to Year 6 (Tables 5.1 and 5.2).

The skills are limited in number, which enables teachers to plan exciting content which is often based on the interests of children. There is greater flexibility in the planning process and this more creative approach also means that there is time to teach the skills more frequently and with greater success. The skills are revisited and revised throughout the whole year so that the children are better able to understand and embed them.

In the Early Years and Year 1 classrooms we also developed our own Continuous Provision Progression Skills curriculum, which maps development

Table 5.1 Whole-School Geography

GEOGRAPHY

Map Skills

EYFS	Y1	Y2	Y3	Y4	Y5	Y6
Draw a journey Navigate a simple journey	Know what a map is Navigate around the school	Explore maps, atlases and globes Navigate around Wisbech Draw maps	Use an index in an atlas/compare to Google Earth Navigate a train/road journey in the UK	Use an index with 2 figure grid reference to locate a specific place Air travel around the world	Use an index with a 4 figure grid reference to locate a specific place Navigate between two specific points – eg geocaching	6 figure grid references Orienteering around a country estate

Locational Knowledge

EYFS	Y1	Y2	Y3	Y4	Y5	Y6
Home and School	Identify physical features of Wisbech Identify human features of Wisbech	Identify physical features of UK Identify human features of UK	Explore physical features of Europe Explore human features of Europe	Explore physical features of the World Explore human features of the world	Study a physical feature of the World Study human features of the world	Study a physical feature of the World Study human features of the world

Table 5.2 Whole-School Science

Science						
Living Things (Animals, Humans and Plants)						
EYFS	Y1	Y2	Y3	Y4	Y5	Y6
Understand the difference between things that are living and things that are not	Understand the differences between humans and animals and plants	Find out the basic needs of animals and plants to survive Talk about life cycles of animals, humans and plants	Understand the different parts of animals, plants and humans and how they differ.	Find out how animals, humans and plants gain and transport their nutrition	Describe the changes to animals, humans and plants as they age Understand how animals, humans and plants adapt to their environment over time	Understand human circulatory system and describe its functions and how diet, exercise, drugs and lifestyle impact on our bodies Describe the process of reproduction in some plants and animals

from nursery to Year 1. These include skills within liquid play, mark making and design and technology skills. From these and the whole school subject skills, we analysed and evaluated the gaps in children's learning and planned our provision accordingly.

Learning themes and topics

In Early Years and Year 1, we have very loose themes so that we are able to incorporate children's interests as well as use a range of high-quality picture books and texts. Through these, children are stimulated to investigate, talk, write and build. We understand the importance of providing 'wow' moments which develop children's curiosity and love of learning. For example, the "Fairy Godmother" from Cinderella came to visit the class, which gave an exciting stimulus for the children to write. We noticed, too, that children are more likely to understand and remember events if they can 'hang' the memory on something which has caused a strong initial response. For example, discovering giant footprints on the playground led to mathematics investigations, various writing opportunities and multiple opportunities in other areas of learning, including constructing a trap in the woodwork area.

Continuous provision and adult inputs

Allowing children to lead their learning means they are more likely to become fully immersed and engrossed in their play. This has implications for adults working alongside them as they must judge when and how to interact with children to develop their thinking. Research undertaken by the Effective Provision of Pre-School Education (EPPE) project noted how often respondents and observers referred to the sharing of thinking and to the way in which some of the interactions were particularly sustained in nature. The coining of the phrase 'sustained shared thinking' was based on this (Sylva et al., 2010).

Bearing all this in mind, the team also decided we would try and limit the number of disruptions which were affecting children's thinking and learning. We looked at our timetable and mapped out how many times we interrupted their play and discussed how to minimise these disruptions. As a result of this, we have no play time in the morning (snack is incorporated into the provision) and any learning interventions are integrated into the continuous provision. Do the children miss playtimes and snack time? In our opinion no, they would much rather continue their play. They have two hours every morning to do this.

Adult inputs or 'teaching' times take place at the beginning and end of each morning. Subjects such as literacy and mathematics are taught to the whole class and children are not divided into groups. We believe that teaching the whole class as one does not put a ceiling on children's learning and all children are exposed to high-quality teaching. However, children who have misconceptions and gaps in their learning are targeted for receiving additional support from adults within the continuous provision times.

Marking, observing and assessing children's work (and providing challenge)

During continuous provision, children are observed and assessed as they had been in the reception class. We expect to observe each child formally twice every week. Their learning is captured through a variety of means including note-taking as well as electronically on tablets. The school policy is to mark work with children 'in the moment', which we do verbally as well as formally. Each child has a folder in which they file any work they have done in their continuous provision session, for example, a design of a model they are going to make or a response to one of the set challenges. There is also a class diary where work is displayed in a portfolio with photographs of children, art work or writing. In this way we capture and show the range of skills that the children have demonstrated.

The children are set two challenges per half term which are linked to the skills they must develop. They choose how to complete these challenges; for example, they may make a model, make a poster or write a booklet in any media they choose. In this way, children are given the choice about how to demonstrate their knowledge and understanding of key skills linked to the current topic. As much of our teaching is interactive and based in play, children have little need to record their learning in books. However, children have literacy exercise books at the beginning of the year and mathematics books are introduced later.

Resources and teaching spaces

We want our children to access the provision in a calm and focused way and the learning environment had to be carefully organised to enable this to happen. Our classrooms and outdoor areas are designed to be safe, enriching and homely. Having visited a local nursery which adopted a Montessori approach and researching this further, we decided to use a range of natural materials and artificial lights to 'soften' the visual aspects of the learning environment. Our children's behaviour was immediately calmed too; they love learning by the light of a lamp in a cosy area. The Reggio Emilia philosophy also promotes the use of natural materials within an aesthetically pleasing environment and it calls the learning space 'the third teacher' because of the impact it has on learning. We want the layout of the classroom and outdoor areas to promote communication and collaboration; it is also important that the learning environment encourages children to explore and be creative. We are very careful in selecting the resources we provide; our resources are mostly natural and provide open-ended material for learning activities, and we ensure that good quality books are available in all areas. Display boards are hessian-backed and walls are neutral and minimally decorated, which also creates a natural, calming backdrop. We use our boards as a celebration of our children's learning and achievements in their independent learning. Resources are stored in natural baskets or neutrally coloured containers (Figures 5.3 and 5.4).

We celebrate children's achievements by displaying their work as it occurs; this immediate reaction shows children that we are proud of their achievements and value the things that they achieve independently. By putting their work on 'celebration boards', we send a strong signal that their work is legitimate and important. This is a powerful motivator. We value our outdoor provision just as much as our indoor provision and believe the outside is our classroom "without a roof". The children are able to move freely from indoors to outdoors as they choose, all day, all year and in all weather, in line with research which has shown the positive benefits in providing free access to different spaces for learning (Bento & Dias, 2017).

Figure 5.3 Classroom before

Figure 5.4 Classroom after

Books everywhere

We believe that when children have the opportunity to explore a range of reading materials, they become curious and consequently stimulated by what they read and see; therefore, we provide magazines and newspapers in the snack and reading areas as well as a range of books around the room. We create 'cosy' places with rugs and cushions which children love and are drawn to. In addition, we take every opportunity to include books in other areas too; for example, books are to be found in the woodwork area (Figure 5.5).

Figure 5.5 Woodwork area

Our challenges

We realise that teaching and learning through continuous provision is not easy; it is an approach that has to be mastered. Throughout this journey both Early Years and Year 1 teachers have faced many challenges. We recognise that without the support from the whole school, this approach can be very daunting to consider. Some of the challenges that we have experienced have been:

- whole school shared understanding of the nature of playful learning
- how do we fit everything in? Quality versus quantity
- timetabling

Whole staff understanding of playful learning

It is fundamental that all school staff have an understanding of 'why play is not just play' and that children are learning through this medium. Therefore, as a school we dedicated time for all staff to come to our classrooms for the morning to observe our children and adults in action. They have witnessed first-hand children learning whilst playing. Children's learning activities are not always immediately obvious to those who are unfamiliar with young children's learning. For example, one KS2 teacher witnessed a child repeatedly 'tapping' against different surfaces outside. The teacher did not recognise the learning that was taking place and asked: "What is he learning? He's just bashing". In fact, the child was creating different sounds, exploring the pitch and sound that each different material made as he tapped it, and he showed that he was being a persevering, motivated and resilient learner through his focused attention. We found that it was helpful to have an experienced Early Years practitioner commentating on children's play as teachers watched so that they became more aware of the learning that was taking place.

Timetable

It is important to be flexible about this. We have changed the timetable at least ten times over the year so that it meets the needs of the children as learners and have sought advice from colleagues working in adjoining years (Figure 5.6).

Autumn Timetable

8.40 – 8.55	Morning task
9.00 – 9.20	Guided Reading
9.20 – 9.30	Literacy input
9.30 – 11.15	Continuous provision Literacy writing in groups
11.15 – 11.50	Maths/phonics
11.50 – 11.55	Ready for lunch
11.55 – 1.05	Lunch
1.05 – 1.30	Maths/phonics
1.30 – 2.30	Continuous provision
2.30 – 2.45	Tidy up
2.45 – 3.00	Reading chest (Adults: Catch Focus Readers)
3.00 – 3.15	How Time Things/ Phonics Recap (Story Time Phonics Video of sound from the day)

Figure 5.6 Autumn timetable

How do we fit everything in? Quality versus quantity

Many teachers have asked how we make sure that the children acquire all the skills and outcomes required by the national curriculum. Given our emphasis on child-led learning, how do we manage to input enough knowledge? Because we have a slimmed down curriculum which emphasises skill acquisition, we have more time to cover this over the year. We believe it is better to cover fewer skills in greater depth over a longer period of time. For example, in the Early Years and Year 1, we have the expectation of two guided writing sessions (writing in small groups) a week instead of five. We firmly believe that this is more beneficial to the children's progress, as they have longer directed teacher time. In this time, misconceptions are addressed, next steps are taught, focus can be made on handwriting and spellings on a 1:1 basis. Children are motivated to write in their self-directed play, producing work which is meaningful and in which they are invested.

In the next section, we discuss the benefits we have found in our new curriculum and why we believe that, through play-based learning, children will make the most progress.

Benefits of continuous provision

We believe that the main benefits of our continuous provision approach can be summarised in the following points:

- improved pupil/teacher interactions
- better support for meeting children's communication and language needs
- responding more effectively to young children's social and emotional needs
- more seamless transition between Early Years and Year 1
- improved learning outcomes
- greater manageability of teachers' workloads and more effective use of teachers' time

High-quality intervention is possible because there is more time and flexibility to focus on key groups and children. Our interactions with children when they are playing enable us to engage with their learning on a personal level and we have also seen improvements in their behaviour since we implemented this approach.

By setting up provision which allows children to engage in open-ended learning, it is possible to adapt and change the classroom to whatever needs your children have. At our school we have high numbers of children who have English as an additional language (EAL), therefore communication and language is an area of development on which we particularly need to focus. We set up learning areas and promote opportunities for children to collaborate and talk as we understand the importance of developing young children's oracy (Mercer, 2018).

As noted at the beginning of this chapter, the transition into Year 1 can be emotionally unsettling for some children, but we have found our transition is now seamless; children are not expected to change their learning style and they continue taking risks and problem solving. In Year 1, we have placed social and emotional needs at the centre of our practice; our school is a very nurturing school, we believe if children are happy, safe and confident then they are ready to learn and more likely to succeed.

We are increasingly aware that children are presenting with higher levels of need in terms of their social and emotional development. By using the learning environment as the 'extra' teacher, we help children to build stronger social and emotional skills and we also support them in becoming more able to articulate their feelings.

Continuous provision allows children to explore, make decisions independently and be curious. By continuing this style of provision in Year 1, we are building on the characteristics of effective learning; playing and exploring, active learning, creating and thinking. These characteristics also builds resilient, independent learners who are confident problem solvers. Surely we want all children to continue these traits throughout their lives and to be successful, lifelong learners.

The levels of attainment reached at the end of Year 1 have not decreased, they have so far remained constant; however, the number of children for whom we close the gap has increased. We believe that this is due to the continuity of practice between reception and Year 1. Research evidence confirms that transition can be a turbulent time and children are often set back by a more formal learning environment. However, by adopting continuous provision in Year 1, transition has been smoother as children have not been expected to change their style of learning.

Our final benefit is improved teachers' wellbeing which, in turn, has positive implications for children. Managing workloads can seem impossible; however, with this model of working, we have found that we have more time to observe children and to adapt the environment and find exciting resources. Our planning centres around developing a long-term plan with open-ended topics and medium-term plans map out the skills to ensure that there is coverage throughout the year. Weekly planning meetings are used to look at children's next steps and to prepare high quality resources and make changes to the physical learning environment. By not writing weekly plans we have found that we are more able to respond to children's interests and respond flexibly to enable them to pursue their ideas (Figure 5.7).

Timeline Showing Year One's Journey into Continuous Provision

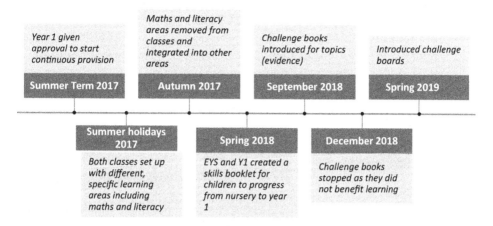

Figure 5.7 The Timeline

Summing up

Lucy and Rachel's story provides us with an individual school's journey of change and how it was implemented over time. Of course, this is only one example and their experiences will be unique to their setting but this example offers an interesting illustration of evidence-informed curriculum design. Using research and theory to guide them, Lucy and Rachel have addressed the concerns they had about meeting children's needs and, as their story shows so vividly, they have carefully considered each step in developing their new curriculum and closely monitored its impact on teaching and learning in their classrooms. They have been willing to change direction when things did not go as they had hoped and their commitment to providing the highest quality provision is evident in all their decision-making. A particularly important aspect of their curriculum design is their consideration of the learning environment, both physical and social, as part of the curriculum.

A final note from Lucy and Rachel

If you are thinking of developing your own practice in a similar way, they would like to offer two key pieces of advice:

- Firstly, consider the learning environment and carefully plan areas and resources to enable children to freely choose and access them. Everything else will follow more easily if this is in place.
- Keep trying different ways of working; continuously evaluate whether you are meeting the needs of the children as well as the expectations of the curriculum.

This journey has not always been easy and we have faced challenges along the way. In many ways it is unfinished. We are still constantly reflecting on our practice in the light of the children's learning outcomes. As a whole team, we continuously evaluate the learning environment and how it impacts on the children's levels of engagement. There has been a transformation in the way in which our children now love learning; the impact on their development, particularly socially and emotionally, has been a pleasure to see. Research confirms that when young children are in environments where learning is occurring within meaningful contexts, if they are given choices and where they are encouraged to follow their own interests, then that is where learning takes place best (Singer, Golinkoff & Hirsh-Pasek, 2006).

References

Alexander, R.J. (ed.) (2010) *Children Their World, Their Education.* Abingdon: Routledge.

Bento, G. and Dias, G. (2017) The importance of outdoor play for young children's healthy development. *Porto Biomedical Journal* 2(5):157–160.

Brooker, L. (2008) *Supporting Transitions in the Early Years.* Maidenhead: Open University Press.

Ephgrave, A. (2017) *Year One in Action.* Abingdon: Routledge.

Fisher, J. (2009) We used to play in foundation, it was more funner': Investigating feelings about transition from foundation stage to year 1. *Early Years* 29(22):131–145.

Mercer, N. (2018) *The Development of Oracy Skills in School-Aged Learners.* Cambridge: CUP.

Singer, D., Golinkoff, R. and Hirsh-Pasek, K. (eds) (2006) *Play=Learning.* New York: Oxford University Press.

Sylva, K., Melhuish, E., Sammons, P., Siraj-Blatchford, I. and Taggart, B. (eds) (2010) *Early Childhood Matters Evidence from the Effective Pre-School and Primary Project.* Abingdon: Routledge.

Trodd, L. (ed.) (2013) *Transitions in the Early Years; Working with Children and Families.* London: Sage.

Vygotsky, L. (1930) *Mind in Society.* Cambridge, MA: Harvard University Press (translated 1978).

Whitebread, D. (2015) Young children learning. In: D. Whitebread and P. Coltman (eds) *Teaching and Learning in the Early Years.* 4th ed. Abingdon: Routledge.

6

Learning to learn from nature

How principles of Harmony in the natural world can guide curriculum design

Richard Dunne and Emilie Martin

Come forth into the light of things,
Let Nature be your teacher.

– William Wordsworth (1798)

Introduction

These two lines are taken from Wordsworth's poem 'The Tables Turned' (Stanza 4, 1798). In it, the poet urges a diligent scholar to leave their books behind and learn, instead, from the wisdom and truth we see in the natural world. The poem sets academic study (which Wordsworth associates with 'toil', 'endless strife' and 'barrenness') and nature (characterised by health and beauty) at opposite ends of the spectrum of learning. The poem's solitary student is presented with a stark choice between learning from books, and engagement with – and learning from – the natural world.

In the context of modern-day primary education in England, teachers and students working and learning within a system which seeks to quantify educational outcomes using a narrow and prescriptive set of descriptors in maths and English may feel they are faced with a similar choice. In reality, of course, the polarities are not so fixed or opposite, and in fact the use of multiple resources will better inform our thinking about how we design a meaningful curriculum and how we make sense of the world in which we live. However, as assessed subjects have increasingly dominated the taught curriculum in English primary schools in recent years, where does nature, and where do natural settings, fit in the education agenda today? How, within the confines of the crowded primary school timetable, can we make space to bring nature into learning – or learning into nature? Where is the natural world afforded the opportunity to be our teacher?

It is our belief, as we will explore in this chapter, that nature and academic enquiry do not exist in a state of polarity. High standards of academic achievement can still be attained and maintained when learning is framed by the principles that exist in the natural world and underpinned by a deep connection with nature. The development of a curriculum that is built upon principles we see at work in the natural world need not stand at odds with a commitment to academic rigour. It is essential that our students' education supports them in developing the skills and knowledge in English, maths and other subjects which are essential to help them have choice rich lives and to succeed, not only in their education but in their lives beyond school (Cantle, 2012). The approach to curriculum development outlined in this chapter does not run counter to the drive for high standards of attainment; rather it represents a new way of structuring teaching and supporting the education of the whole person. If we, as educators, are to do more than simply inculcate subject-specific skills and knowledge, it is imperative that the education we offer to our students is equally rooted in values, capacities and principles that are relevant to the world and the time in which we live, as it is to teaching the subject-specific skills and content that are enshrined in the National Curriculum.

This view of the wider purpose of education is articulated in the United Nation's *GE06 Healthy Planet Healthy People* report (2019), which highlights the role of key competencies linked to education for sustainable development in contributing to the development of sustainability-minded citizens. Critical and systems thinking, collaboration and self-awareness are listed among the examples of these competencies and the importance of sustainability-oriented values and motivations is also referenced. The report goes on to emphasise that in order for education for sustainable development to have impact, its principles must permeate the taught and non-taught curricula, rather than being seen as an add-on (United Nations, 2019). This means that it must be taught by teachers and enacted within the values and community in which the children will learn and grow. It is about extending the learning beyond the classroom, into nature, into their local and global world and into their communities. We have seen how learning is enriched by such a cohesive and purposeful approach to education. By developing a curriculum which is built upon the principles we see in nature and which promotes engagement with the issues that threaten the health of our planet (and, therefore, our selves), we offer students an education which may better equip them to lead on the issues which threaten our collective wellbeing, both now and in the future. Box 6.1 brings together the key principles of Harmony to which we refer throughout the chapter.

Box 6.1: Principles of Harmony

The principles of Harmony which are referred to throughout this chapter, and upon which the curriculum development work at Ashley C of E Primary School are based, can be thought of as natural laws that maintain the dynamic balance and wellbeing of the natural world (Dunne, 2019). They are drawn from the ideas contained in the book *Harmony: A new way of looking at our world* by HRH The Prince of Wales, Ian Skelly and Tony Juniper (2010). We have provided as a preface to this chapter a short overview of the seven principles that are the foundation for the development of a Harmony curriculum. These are:

The principle of the cycle

Cycles in nature are self-sustaining and self-regulating. When we apply what we learn from these never-ending, self-limiting cycles to our own lives and work, we are better placed to adopt more sustainable practices.

The principle of interdependence

All life on Earth is wholly interconnected. When we appreciate this, we begin to see that our actions and choices have consequences which may affect the wellbeing of individuals, communities and systems beyond ourselves.

The principle of health

Our wellbeing is linked to the wellbeing of the natural world. By understanding this, we may be more motivated to live in a way which maintains our health alongside the health of our planet and increase our engagement with nature.

The principle of diversity

Diversity in the natural world sustains life and brings strength and resilience to a system. We can apply what we learn about diversity in nature to improve practices in specific fields of work, such as farming, as well as find ways to appreciate the value of diversity in our own relationships.

The principle of geometry

We see repeating patterns and proportions everywhere in nature. By exploring these patterns and proportions, and by discovering that they are also present in us as much as around us, we understand that we *are* nature.

The principle of adaptation

There are countless examples in nature of how living things adapt to their environment. When we connect more fully with our localities and communities, we can contribute to the world immediately around us for the benefit of all.

The principle of oneness

All principles of Harmony are linked. We may focus on each principle separately to better understand it, but each is part of the same whole. There is strength to be gained from understanding that just as all life on this planet is part of a greater system, so we are part of something greater than ourselves – something which could be considered a more spiritual oneness.

A key cultural value in building a curriculum on these principles is the strongly held view that humans are part of nature and do not stand apart from it. As Ian Skelly, a co-author of *Harmony: A new way of looking at our world*, told the authors of this chapter:

> If you were to ask me what this all comes down to, I would say that to look at the world through the prism of Harmony requires that we do not see humanity as standing apart from nature, nor that nature is merely a collection of individual mechanical parts. Rather, it is a complex whole. In other words, rather than being a part of nature, we are nature – an entirely interconnected, spiritually rooted complexity. If we understand this, we may begin to shift our outlook from one that is reductive and mechanistic to one that is more balanced and much more integrated with nature's complexity, recognizing the importance not just of building up our financial capital, but how to nurture our social and community capital and, ultimately, protect nature's capital.

Whilst this chapter focuses on the UK context and in one school, the increasing concern about climate change, the decimation of the natural world through human activity and the diaspora that has interconnected people across the globe in various ways, both positive and negative, emphasise the point. We are nature. But how does this translate into the UK primary school context? How do teachers enable this type of curricula?

Bringing learning and nature together

The UK has a 'rich tradition' of promoting young people's engagement with the natural environment dating back to the 19th century, encompassing Margaret McMillan's *open air movement* and Montessori pre-school education, to name but two influential approaches (Cree and McCree, 2012). The now well-known Forest School Movement, which takes its inspiration from Danish pre-school approaches to learning, can be traced back to 1993 in the UK. Today, the Forest School Association has 1,700 members, up from just 200 five years ago. Organisations such as Beach Schools South West are doing for learning in coastal settings what the Forest School Association has done for learning in woodlands. Meanwhile, organisations such as the Council for Learning Outside the Classroom and initiatives such as the Natural Connections Demonstration Project (a four-year collaboration between Natural England, Defra, Historic England and the University of Plymouth, which concluded in 2016) have sought to promote and quantify the impact of learning in natural settings, respectively.

Natural England's final report on the impact of the Natural Connections project reveals a range of positive outcomes of learning in the natural environment for students. Of the schools surveyed, 95% said learning in the natural environment had a positive impact on students' enjoyment of lessons and 92% reported a positive impact on students' health, wellbeing and engagement with learning.

Meanwhile, 93% of schools noted a positive impact in students' social skills and 85% reported a positive impact on behaviour. Measured against specifically academic criteria, Natural England also cites research showing that:

> School students engaged in learning in natural environments have been found to have higher achievement (in comparison to their peers or projected attainment) in reading, mathematics, science and social studies, exhibiting enhanced progress in physical education and drama, and a greater motivation for studying science.
>
> *(Natural England, 2016)*

These figures help to illustrate some of the ways in which learning in the natural environment benefits young people. But what would the benefits be if we took education beyond learning *in* nature, even beyond learning *about* nature to embrace an education based on learning *from* nature? This educational engagement with the natural world is central to the work of a primary school that we will refer to throughout this chapter – a school that is developing its own distinctive curriculum. It is a curriculum inspired by principles that maintain order, wellbeing and Harmony in the natural world, a curriculum that is being developed to encourage students to form a deep connection with – and reverence for – nature, to learn from it and to develop a sense of agency and purpose that will allow them to become stewards of the natural world.

Before we look at the curriculum development work the school is engaged in, let us turn our attention briefly to the context for this school's work.

Adaptation in the education system

Concerns about the narrowing of the taught curriculum in primary and secondary schools as a result of the standards agenda – with its focus on high-stakes assessment and progress data – have been well documented (Alexander, 2010). As well as impoverishing the educational experience of individual students, the constraining of the curriculum may have damaging implications for our collective future prosperity. Writing about the impact of high-stakes assessment on the taught curriculum in US schools, Berliner (2011) argues that cuts of up to one third in the teaching time devoted to subjects such as social studies, science, physical education, art and music, may have a negative effect on students' participation in democracy, their development as responsible citizens, their creative thinking skills and ultimately their contribution to the economy and society as a whole.

> The dominance of testing as part of American and British school reform policies insures that many of the skills thought to be most useful in the twenty-first century will not be taught. Thus, students and their national economies will suffer when nations rely too heavily on high stakes testing to improve their schools.
>
> *(Berliner, 2011)*

Purpose in education

In England, the need for increased breadth and balance in the curriculum is also recognised, not least (some might say, belatedly) by Her Majesty's Inspectorate, Ofsted. Commenting on the narrowing of the curriculum, Her Majesty's Chief Inspector, Amanda Spielman, notes:

> Across the whole education sector, a mentality of "what's measured is what gets done" trumps the true purpose of education, and curriculum thinking – the consideration of what needs to be taught and learned for a full education – has been eroded.
>
> *(Spielman, 2018)*

In response to this, Ofsted's revised framework for inspection places greater emphasis on the quality of the curriculum that educational settings either adopt, adapt or develop. On the face of it, this seems encouraging, a nod to the importance of schools' and educators' reflections on what they teach – and why. However, the objectives relating to Quality of Education in Ofsted's draft framework, effective from September 2019, state that a school's curriculum should be "coherently planned and sequenced towards cumulatively sufficient knowledge and skills for future learning and employment". The criteria inspectors will use to arrive at judgements about the impact of an educational setting's quality of education will assess whether "learners are ready for the next stage of education, employment or training" (Ofsted, 2019).

We would argue that by enshrining in inspection descriptors this rather short-term, linear view of education as a process that exists simply to equip young people with the tools they need to progress to the next stage of their educational journey, a very valuable opportunity has been missed. While having the skills needed to succeed in further study and to secure a job are, of course, important outcomes of education, an equally pressing goal is that young people's education enables them to engage with – and lead on – the environmental issues that threaten the fabric of life on Earth. If one considers the University of Cambridge's visionary commitment to reducing the effects of climate change through its interdisciplinary research and advocacy (www.zero.cam.ac.uk), we note that education is also about the preservation of the natural world. The education we provide should allow them the opportunity to explore the consequences of the choices they each make in their daily lives and to reflect on how they want to live, how they want to act and how they want to be.

This is acknowledged by the UN in its Sustainable Development Goals, which define sustainable development as "development that meets the needs of the present without compromising the ability of future generations to meet their own needs". Many of the targets within Sustainable Development Goal 4, which relates to Quality Education, focus on equal access to an education that equips the learner with the academic, technical or vocational skills needed for employment. However, Target 4.7 specifically states that education should equip learners with, "the knowledge and skills needed to promote sustainable development, including, among others, through education for sustainable development and sustainable lifestyles" (UN Sustainable Development Goals, retrieved online May 2019).

In short, our planet – and all life on it – needs people who live well in their own place. It needs people of moral courage willing to join the fight to make the world more habitable and humane. And these needs have little to do with success as most Western cultures have defined it (Orr, 1991). A critical skill that is largely absent from the National Curriculum, but which is – and which is increasingly likely to be – of utmost importance to our young people, is the notion of environmental literacy.

The Cambridge Primary Review Trust highlighted the importance of *experiencing* nature and of *engaging with* the natural world first-hand in developing what Orr (1991) described as 'ecological literacy' almost 30 years ago. We know that children care about the natural world and are intuitively fascinated by it: "There is considerable evidence of children's awareness of issues like climate change and the need to recycle materials" (Alexander and Hargreaves, 2007). However, typically awareness of environmental issues comes not from direct engagement with the environment itself but from a more passive and indirect understanding of these issues. Direct interaction with the natural environment appears to be increasingly absent in children's lives and this new phenomenon gives rise to concern because such experiences are essential in developing children's knowledge and understanding of the world (Bourn, Hunt, Blum, and Lawson, 2016).

As educators, then, we must be mindful (even if Ofsted may not be) of the skills that will allow our young people to thrive in the 21st century and which will enable them to develop a different relationship with the natural world, one that is based upon ways of living that work in harmony with nature. The Organization for Economic Cooperation and Development (OECD) is also turning its attention to the skills that will best equip young people globally for success in the world they will inhabit as adults – skills such as co-operation, critical thinking, achievement, motivation and persistence. This is the context in which we need to adapt and develop our curriculum and in which the curriculum development work at Ashley Church of England Primary school is taking place.

Learning to thrive

The starting point for this new way of learning is to explore the curriculum in relation to principles of Harmony that maintain a dynamic and healthy balance in the natural world. These principles teach us how the natural world works and has worked for millions of years (refer to Box 6.1). They remind us that sustainable systems and practices can be found everywhere in nature. The more we use them to guide and inform our own understanding of how the world works, the more we, too, will learn to live sustainably and well.

For example, one of these principles – the principle of adaptation – shows us how species in the natural world change and evolve over time in order to flourish and thrive. This can take many forms, from the structural adaptation that allows desert-dwelling cacti and succulents to store water to behavioural adaptation that sees animals migrate to feed or breed more successfully. We now find ourselves at a point where the education we offer our young people must adapt in order for them to thrive and engage with the urgent environmental problems that threaten their future. We need a new approach to education that helps young people to see the world differently and to appreciate the role they can play in ensuring we live in harmony with it – that we are indeed nature.

The curriculum development work at Ashley School is based on seven principles of Harmony that can be found in the natural world. Alongside the principle of adaptation are six further principles: the principles of the cycle, interdependence, geometry, diversity, health and oneness. If we consider the natural world as a self-sustaining system, each principle provides a different perspective on the same whole. Each gives us a different way of seeing and understanding how this remarkable, complex system works. And each opens up opportunities to explore learning in new and exciting ways. In this way, it is the principles of nature's Harmony that are the starting point for the learning, not schemes of work and not the curriculum folder. It is these principles that give learning a new context.

At Ashley School, the learning in each year group is planned around a different principle of Harmony each half term so that in every year group, the children explore each of the principles once during the academic year. By the end of Year 6, then, we can see that each child will have explored each of the principles of Harmony the school has selected as the basis for learning, a total of seven times through seven different learning enquiries. If we take the principle of the cycle as an example, we can map out a child's exploration of this principle through their learning as they progress through primary school and see at once how the complexity of this exploration can be developed. In the summer term, the Reception children at Ashley School learn about the creatures that live outside their classroom and about farm animals. As part of this learning, they look at the lifecycle of butterflies, frogs and chickens, and their extraordinary metamorphosis from one form to another. By Year 3, children at the school learn about the life cycle of native trees and the role of seeds in sustaining a species. In Year 4, they learn about the never-ending orbits of the planets around the sun or the lunar cycle and its impact on the tides. A year later, children in Year 5 explore the water cycle and its crucial role in sustaining life on Earth. Beyond this learning *about* the principle of the cycle, the children are also encouraged to learn *from* it. If nature is cyclical, then what does that mean in terms of the way we live? In a world of finite resources, how can we ensure our practices are cyclical, too?

Reflections on learning

The importance of supporting the children in reflecting on what they have learnt and how it can be applied in the context of their own lives is key to this approach to learning and planning at the school. When the children in Year 3 explore the principle of interdependence by learning how a rainforest or a local woodland exists as an ecosystem, they learn how every element within the system has a value and a role to play. They also reflect upon what happens when one element within this system is threatened, and what the nature of these threats might be. Similarly, in Year 5, the children look at the ocean and how each individual species enables the whole system to work in a constantly dynamic flow of relationships. Also planned into the learning is the impact of humans on this underwater world and what we are doing to damage or degrade such an abundant, yet fragile system. As part of their learning, the children reflect on how social ecosystems in the form of human communities work together and on the importance of the diverse roles and contributions of different individuals within these social groups.

Importantly, in appreciating how all life is interconnected, the children start to consider the way they want to live and to become more discerning about the choices they make. When, for example, we have a better understanding of the hugely negative impact that industrial farming systems have on the health of our soil, air and water, we are better placed to find ways to work with nature, not against it. The more we look to nature and learn how it works and has worked so successfully for so long, the more we will find the solutions to a more sustainable future ourselves. This has led Ashley School to commit only to serve organic school meals and to think creatively about how we can make that happen.

A sense of place

In all this, we need to give learning a strong sense of place, of local context. As we have already referenced, nature is brilliantly adapted to its place; its designs and forms have evolved over millions of years to enable species to survive and thrive in their habitats. Traditional cultures work in the same way, developing practices that use local materials and work with the land to support a sustainable way of life. We still have so much to learn from their practices – they are models of Harmony at work.

By providing opportunities for students to learn to live well in their place by adapting and applying their thinking to the place in which they live, we can open up all sorts of exciting potential for partnerships beyond the school. These partnerships can enrich learning and enable expertise to be passed on from one generation to the next. When students engage in projects that connect them to their place and their community, they may be more likely to want to contribute to it as they grow up. When we adapt learning to a local context, we help students develop an identity to place and a sense of belonging. 'Living well in our places' illustrates this approach in practice.

Living well in our places

In the Autumn Term, the children in Year 5 explore the learning enquiry – *What journey does a river take?* – linked to the principle of the cycle. As the River Thames is a short walk away from the school, the children visit the river to observe its features at this stage in its journey from source to sea. Wherever possible, the learning across all subjects is linked to this learning enquiry throughout the half term.

In science, the children learn about the water cycle and the influence this has on the life of a river, while in geography they find out how water is treated to make it safe to drink. There is plenty to support this aspect of their learning locally as there are several reservoirs and water treatment plants close to the school, and this ties in nicely with learning about water conservation and the responsible use of water. In English, the children write poetry about water, information texts about the different parts of a river, including those found in the local area, and they research the issue surrounding our consumption of bottled versus tap water and write persuasive letters on this topic.

As areas close to the school were affected by flooding in January 2014, the children also learn what happens when a river floods and the impact this has on the population affected. They are visited by local people whose houses or businesses were flooded and reflect on how we need to adapt our lifestyles and our choices to lessen the impact of flooding, both in the UK and in other areas of the world.

Planning back to front

So how is this approach to learning planned out? In effect, it is an approach that works back to front. Teachers start with the enquiry question – a big question that frames the half-term's learning. This enquiry question is often based on the initial conversations the staff have had with the children about what they are interested in learning when studying a particular topic. Each enquiry question also relates to one of the six principles of Harmony that provide the context for learning each year – the cycle, interdependence, diversity, adaptation, health and oneness. The seventh principle – the principle of geometry – is explored throughout every learning enquiry as a cross-cutting strand in the school's curriculum.

The staff then looks at what the outcome of the half-term's enquiry could be. This might be some kind of performance, exhibition, recital or presentation that will give purpose and direction to the learning. This is not an add-on; it is not about creating more work. Rather, it is a way for the children to build towards a meaningful outcome, just as nature does. For example, when the children in Year 6 learn about First World War poets, they conclude their enquiry by writing, decorating and reciting their own poems about the concepts of war and peace to parents and family. When the children in Year 1 learn about local wildflowers, they make wildflower books and share them with the Year 2 children at the end of the first half-term of the Summer Term. In return and with reference to the hexagonal bee books they have made, the Year 2 children teach their Year 1 friends about bee colonies and the role they play in a healthy ecosystem. These Great Works – as the school calls them – give a purpose to the children's learning and help them to develop a sense of their own agency that comes from sharing the outcomes of their work. The school wants its students to value these end-of-project outcomes as something great, something memorable, something that instils in them a real sense of self-worth and confidence. They are projects that help the children to flourish.

Once the Great Work has been agreed, it is then time to build the learning journey through weekly questions that will provide the focus for each week. The geometry acts as a starter or introduction to the learning for that week and the English and maths skills are practised and then applied in relation to the weekly question. Wherever possible, foundation subjects will also be taught with reference to the enquiry. For the most part this works. The intention is that as much of the learning as possible has relevance to the wider enquiry. The school teaches enquiries that are either science-based, geography-based or history-based and this enables us to focus on quality over quantity with two enquiries per year for each of these three subjects.

The geometry has become a key feature of the learning. Not only does it provide a new lens through which to see and understand the world, it helps the children to draw the patterns of nature with increasing confidence and in increasing complexity. The children often start their geometry work with short sketches to get their eye in before working on their geometric shapes. They begin to notice how patterns in nature are repeated in a range of forms from the micro to the macro, and they learn that the patterns in the world around them exist in them, too. This gives them a very different perspective on the world and their place within it. The more the children engage with this geometry, the more their attention to detail develops, the more the quality of their work improves and the more their self-esteem flourishes.

Outcomes of a Harmony curriculum

The introduction of a Harmony curriculum at Ashley School is still relatively recent. The first cohort of children at the school whose learning will have followed this curriculum throughout the entirety of their primary schooling will not finish Year 6 until the summer of 2023.

Unsurprisingly, then, research into the outcomes of this curriculum is still at an early stage. However, studies involving the children and staff at the school already highlight some key themes emerging from this distinctive approach to learning. Taking as an example learning linked to the principle of geometry, there have been reported improvements in children's fine motor skills, their attention to detail and resilience in learning, better concentration and mindfulness and increased self-esteem. These are skills which may not be as easily quantifiable as, for example, calculation skills in maths or reading comprehension, but which are just as important to academic – and indeed, lifelong – success.

The following are comments from Ashley School teachers about the skills the children are developing as a result of their geometry learning:

> The children have their own expectations about what they want their learning to look like. If it hasn't worked out the way they want it to, they ask to do it again. But in another subject, you might not have seen before the same level of care taken by the same child. There's an element of self-regulation there.
>
> *(Tasha, Year 4 teacher)*

> Children who find other learning quite tricky can flourish in these activities. And they know that this learning has as high priority in our school.
>
> *(Louise, Year 5 teacher)*

In the academic year 2017–2018, the school was one of the subjects of a study by researchers at Canterbury Christ Church University as a school developing its curriculum around elements of earth education. The study's authors describe a "holistic and multi-layered approach" to Harmony education that involves the whole school community, and identify two outcomes of this approach as being: firstly, that the children have a sense of environmental leadership and steward-ship; and secondly, that they have an understanding of our dependence upon the natural world.

This is borne out in conversation with the children themselves, and in their reflections on their learning. For example, at the end of their learning enquiry "How can we ensure our oceans stay amazing?", the children in Year 5 were asked to draw on their learning throughout the half term to respond to the enquiry question. Sam, age 10, said: "Plastic rubbish is killing the creatures of the ocean. Because all the creatures are connected to each other, if we kill the creatures, the food chain will be destroyed. We need to work out how to stop this". In giving this response, he shows an understanding of the environmental impact of human behaviour on sea life and of the highly interconnected nature of all living things. However, he also goes on to say that it is us who must find solutions to this problem.

Other examples of the children's comments, which highlight their under-standing of different principles of Harmony and the relevance they have to their own lives, are given below:

> I have learnt that if you live with nature, you can live almost anywhere. The Inuit give to mother nature, but also take so it is an endless cycle.
>
> *(Lance, Year 6)*

If you didn't have diversity in the landscape on Earth, all the wildlife would be the same. There are things in nature that people need and if we didn't have a diverse planet we wouldn't have all the different resources.

(Olivia, Year 4)

You find examples in nature of how living things have adapted or changed to survive. It shows you how we need to adapt our lives and the way we live to make things better for everyone. We can make one small change and it will improve things for people in other parts of the world.

(Meghan, Year 6)

A cycle never stops. It never ends. It repeats itself in a chain or like a circle unless something interrupts it. When a cycle is interrupted, the whole cycle breaks.

(Eden, Year 5)

Developing this approach in other schools

The curriculum development work around principles of Harmony at Ashley School has not gone unnoticed; other schools are now applying principles of Harmony to their own curriculum development work. One such school is South Farnborough Infants, a two-form entry infant school with approximately 330 children on-roll. As at Ashley, there is a tradition of education focused on sustainability at South Farnborough Infant School and the application of principles of Harmony to learning is given a high priority.

The approach to building learning around principles of Harmony at South Farnborough differs from the approach taken at Ashley School. At the Walton-on-Thames school, principles of Harmony have been matched and mapped to individual enquiries of learning so that children in each year group explore each of the principles the school has selected as the basis for learning once each academic year. At South Farnborough, in contrast, principles of Harmony still underpin learning, but teachers draw on whichever principles they feel fit best with the focus for enquiry that half term – or even that week. The children could, therefore, explore an aspect of each principle of Harmony each half term.

South Farnborough Infant School Headteacher Helen Fletcher-Davis explains that one of the school's main objectives in developing its own Harmony curriculum is to help the children understand that they are connected to the wider world, and to foster in them an understanding of their own agency and ability to change things for the better, "We want to encourage the children to look beyond themselves at the wider world that they will one day play a greater part in. Integrating Harmony principles into learning helps achieve this", said Helen.

Concluding thoughts

In this chapter, we have offered an example of what a curriculum which connects children more deeply to the natural world – and which empowers them to effect positive change –might look like. We have also explained why it is of such importance that the education we offer our young people adapts to help them develop the knowledge and skills they will need to engage with the issues that threaten their ability to thrive. Some of our teachers have commented:

> Children develop a really good understanding of their place in the world and the impact of people's choices.

> Children are developing and embedding a sense of moral purpose with regards to guardianship of their world.

Humankind – and indeed all life on Earth – has great challenges ahead and we need a different model of education to enable us to address them properly; the current model is not fit for this purpose. It is not enough simply to learn about sustainability in a classroom. At a time when the UK Government has announced a climate emergency, education should be at the forefront of those leading the change in outlook and developing the practices needed to address this emergency. We need students to understand that nature provides us with the best model for sustainable practices in the form of the principles that maintain harmony, health and balance in the natural world. We need students to explore issues of sustainability in a joined-up, coherent way and apply their subject knowledge and skills to projects which are purposeful and meaningful. Our students need to see themselves as change-makers and to see the outcomes of their education as having relevance to their lives and their future. The more we realise their potential through this approach, the better.

We can draw out four key aspects to the Harmony curriculum being developed at Ashley School, which might prove useful to other schools and educators looking to embark upon a similar journey in curriculum design. Firstly, students have the opportunity to develop a deep connection with nature, learning from the natural world, developing a reverence for it and understanding how principles of Harmony in nature can inspire the way we choose to live and to be. Secondly, by framing learning within principles of Harmony, the learning process itself becomes more cohesive, coherent and purposeful. Thirdly, by supporting students in planning projects which are an expression of their reflections on their learning, they are able to see that their learning has purpose and to develop a sense of ownership of that learning. Lastly, but running through all of this, teaching and learning at the school has an emphasis on locality. This helps to make tangible for students the concepts they explore in their learning. The knowledge they already have about their local river, for example, provides them with a starting point for their learning about rivers further afield. The issues surrounding litter and other forms of pollution – and its effect on wildlife – is as relevant to the waterway that is familiar to them as it is to other bodies of freshwater. The interweaving of local partners into the curriculum opens the students' eyes to the skills and knowledge that exist on their doorstep and which can enrich their learning and their lives. And by supporting students in taking the lead in bringing about positive change – however small – in their local area, they begin to see that they have the power and ability to act to change the things that cause them concern. They start to become the environmental stewards and leaders of the future.

We are now seeing the emergence of a network of similarly minded schools and organisations, both within the UK and beyond, who are seeking to develop a Harmony approach in their own settings. This is not an undertaking to be embarked upon lightly, as it involves a radically new approach to teaching and to learning, making nature the teacher in order to ensure our own future health and prosperity, and the health and prosperity of the natural world, of which we are such an integral part. We started with Wordsworth and we end with another William. William Blake, the visionary poet of the 18th century, wrote that,

> The tree which moves some to tears of joy is in the eyes of others only a green thing that stands in the way. Some see nature all ridicule and deformity… and some scarce see nature at all. But to the eyes of the man of imagination, nature is imagination itself.
>
> *(Blake, 1799: from a letter he wrote to a Reverend John Trusler*
> *in the summer of 1799, sourced online May 2019)*

Surely it is time to focus on education that fulfils the whole child, in connection with nature, and as nature? As with Blake, we envision a more hopeful future through a meaningful experience of education which connects students to the world in which they live and the role they can play in sustaining it.

To learn more about how principles of Harmony are being applied in practice, visit www.theharmonyproject.org.uk.

Further reading

Alexander, R. (Ed.) (2010) *Children, Their World, Their Education: Findings and Recommendations of the Cambridge Primary Review.* London: Routledge.

Alexander, R. and Hargreaves, L. (2007) *The Commuity Soundings: The Primary Review Regional Witness Sessions.* Cambridge: Faculty of Education, University of Cambridge.

Berliner, D. (2011) Rational Responses to High Stakes Testing: The case of curriculum narrowing and the harm that follows. *Cambridge Journal of Education*, 41(3), 287–302.

Blake, W. (1799) A personal letter written to Reverend John Trusler in the summer of 1799, sourced online May 2019 Available at https://www.bra inpickings.org/2016/07/14/william-blake-john-trusler-letter [accessed 01/04/2020].

Bourn, D., Hunt, F., Blum, N. and Lawson, H. (2016) *Primary Education for Global Learning and Sustainability*. York: Cambridge Primary Review Trust.

Cantle, T. (2012) *Interculturalism: The New Era of Cohesion and Diversity*. Basingstoke: Palgrave MacMillan.

Cree, J. and McCree, M. (2012) History of the Roots of Forest School in the UK (Part 1). *Horizons*, 60(Winter), 32–34.

Dunne, R. (2019) *Harmony: A New Way of Looking at and Learning About Our World. A Teacher's Guide to Purposeful Learning*. Bristol: The Harmony Project/ Sustainable Food Trust.

HRH The Prince of Wales, Juniper, T. and Skelly, I. (2010) *Harmony: A New Way of Looking at Our World*. Blue Door: Harper Collins.

Natural England (2016) *Natural Connections Demonstration Project: Final Report*. London: Natural England.

Ofsted (2019) *The Education Inspection Framework*. London: Ofsted.

Orr, D.W. (1991) *The Economics of Conservation. Conservation Education*, 5(4), 439–441.

Spielman, A. (2018) *Speech launching the Ofsted Annual Report 2017/2018*. Published online: available at https://www.gov.uk/government/speec hes/amanda-spielman-launches-ofsteds-annual-report-201718 [accessed 02/04/2020].

United Nations (2019) *United Nations Sustainable Development Goals*. Available at: https://sustainabledevelopment.un.org/?menu=1300 [accessed 02/04/2020].

United Nations Environment (2019) *Global Environment Outlook: GEO6 Healthy Planet, Healthy People*. Cambridge: Cambridge University Press.

Wordsworth, W. and Coleridge, S.T. (1798) *Lyrical Ballads with a Few Other Poems*. London: J. and A. Arch.

7

Knowing about and acting globally in everyday classrooms

Susan Lee Robertson and Ana Mocanu

Inserting the global into classroom practices

Over the years, teachers have been acutely aware of the global in their class-rooms, especially when teaching in schools with diverse ethnic populations. It would not be uncommon for a school's reception area to proudly hang a map of the global showing how many nationalities there were on the school's roll. Throughout the 1980s and 90s in countries like the UK, Canada and Australia, teachers could also point to what were called multicultural policies aimed at responding to this kind of cultural diversity. Such policies, however, were often critiqued as gestural, especially when centred on a narrow range of aspects of a culture, such as national foods and ethnic costumes.

A great deal is again being made of the need to insert 'the global' into the curriculum in schools around the world to enable learners to acquire those knowledges, skills and values so as to engage with pressing societal and environmental challenges. Many of these challenges are seen as cultural; for example, our attitudes toward others who we see as different from ourselves, our behaviour toward the environment and a culture of individualism. A series of mappings, assessment frameworks and templates have been launched with a view to changing what it is that schools and teachers might do to create new understandings and behaviours (cf. Bourn et al., 2016; OECD, 2018). Acquiring global learning, developing global competences or promoting global citizenship is viewed in these reports as a way of promoting a more inclusive world through education.

We agree education has an important role to play. However, we argue that there are major issues with the current approaches because of simplistic under-standings of the role of culture in global processes and challenges. We suggest a different way forward so that learners and teachers might encounter the global in a positive and transformative way.

We begin by exploring the reasons why 'the global' is being reemphasised, noting a shift in its framing compared to the 1990s. We then examine a suite of initiatives being promoted to address global learning and citizenship. We look at recent mappings of 'global citizenship education' in national settings, before turning Target 4.7 of the Sustainable Development Goals (SDG) to be realised by 2030, United Nations Education, Scientific and Cultural Organization (UNESCO) Global Citizenship Education (GCED), the global competence assessment framework, and the Organization for Economic Cooperation and Development (OECD). We tease out the assumptions underpinning different initiatives, and particularly how culture, and cultural change, is understood.

In the final section of this chapter, we sketch out a series of question-driven steps teachers might use to spark conversations and develop initiatives with learners in the classroom. These questions are aimed at engaging students in a dialogue in the classroom and beyond around pressing social and environmental issues. Such issues demand cultural and intercultural knowledge, skills and practices if they are to lead to a transformation in students' views and behaviours around diverse ways of knowing and being.

Why promote 'the global' now?

Throughout the 1990s, globalisation was mobilised as either a solution to a myriad of cultural, political and economic issues within nation states, or a force to be reckoned with. As a solution, globalisation was seen as creating global interconnections, new efficiencies through market integration and a global society. As a force to be reckoned with, globalisation was represented as a juggernaut that steamrollered national governments into accepting a new competitive world order.

By the early 2000s, more critical perspectives on globalisation began to emerge. Globalisation was seen not as a single unified phenomenon but rather "a syndrome of processes and activities" which had become normalised as a "dominant ideology that joins with neoliberalism to extol the virtues of individualism, efficiency, competition and minimal state intervention in the economy" (Mittelman, 2004, p. 5). However, the promise of neoliberalism, whose instruments were argued to enable all boats to rise, were increasingly in question. As early as 2008, an OECD report *Growing Unequal?* flagged rising income inequalities and poverty in OECD countries and beyond. Yet the OECD was insistent that countries should embrace, rather than retreat from, greater integration into the global world order. What was needed, the OECD argued, was a more adequate statistical infrastructure to monitor changes in poverty and income inequality over time (OECD, 2008, p. 3).

In 2011, the OECD returned to the issue of growing global inequalities in *Divided We Stand* (OECD: 2011). They noted that income inequalities had already begun to increase in the UK and the USA in the early 1980s (p. 22), and that this pattern had become more widespread by the 2000s, including in those regarded as 'low-inequality' countries: Germany, Sweden and Denmark.

However, again the OECD Report was equivocal as to the determining role of neoliberal ideas (p. 24), arguing the evidence was mixed. However, they did agree that policy choices, regulations and institutional arrangements mattered (OECD, 2011, p. 26).

A chorus of voices, including well-known economists (cf. Piketty, 2014), added to the volume of evidence that neoliberal policies had effects. The accumulated consequences of speculative financial capital, low levels of corporate taxation, the rise of a managerial elite, and a small group of super rich was contrasted with middle and low-income earners who now had declining incomes, precarious work and a smaller share of global wealth. This, in turn, undermined the necessary social cohesion at the base of an inclusive society as well as resources to fund public services like education.

According to Sennett (2006), a key culprit in the rise of inequalities and social unrest emerged out of the culture of the new capitalism. He pointed to the rampant promotion of individualism, narrow-minded entrepreneurship and the replacement of meritocracy with the idea of talent. In combination, these attributes fostered individual competitivism and the view that winning was everything. But winning is premised on someone losing, in turn reinforcing new social differences. When some groups come to understand themselves as losing out economically and socially, new resentments as to who is to blame have surfaced (Cohen, 2019). Rather than point their finger at the pernicious effects of neoliberal policies, those who have been left behind have turned on those who are different – migrants, ethnic groups, gypsies and travellers – as the cause of their loss in status.

Boven and Wille (2017) point to a new education cleavage emerging in many countries across Europe. They place on one side a cosmopolitan, well-educated, elite, and on the other those whose education experiences are limited, and whose worldviews are shaped by a parochial media and jingoistic politics.

Such cleavages have become a breeding ground for conflict and resentment amongst those who have been on the sharp end of redistribution and recognition failures. They have also been fuelled by the war on terror, the rise of Islam, conflict in the Middle East and the mass movement of refugees across the surrounding borders. Close to 70 million forcibly displaced people have found themselves on the move toward Europe, or uneasily incorporated into its communities. The rise of populist politicians and politics – from Trump in the United States, to the Brexit vote in the UK and right-wing movements in Europe – are all manifestations of deeper challenges facing many societies and their communities.

If the rights of forced immigrants and asylum seekers has divided communities, so too has the future of the planet around claims regarding the extinction of many of the earth's species, fossil fuel depletion, evidence of climate change and the sustainability of current models of economic development. This has divided experts, countries and generations. However, earth-orbiting satellites and other technological advances have enabled scientists to see the big picture, collecting many different types of information about the planet and its climate on a global scale. Melting glaciers, shrinking ice-sheets, warming oceans and a rise in sea levels can be detected and measured. This has galvanised a younger generation of school children (e.g. Extinction Rebellion) who in 2018 and 2019 have become active as climate change protestors and put the older generation on notice. Such concerns reinforce the need to include sustainability in education's global agendas.

So what is to be done, and what are the implications for teachers in schools? For sure education is regarded as part of the solution to these global problems. But much will depend on how these issues are conceptualised in curriculum materials, and how teachers engage pedagogically with these in their classrooms.

New education solutions to global problems

In his chapter entitled 'Pedagogy for a runaway world', Alexander makes the following remark:

> if we contemplate the increasing fragility, inequality, and instability of our world as a whole, and believe that these are not only unacceptable in themselves but are also, as a matter of fact, contrary to the national interest – because like first-class passengers in an aircraft crash, in a global catastrophe no country remains immune – then education will need to espouse very different priorities: moral no less than economic, holistic rather than fragmented, and collective rather than individualistic.
>
> *(2008, p. 127)*

We agree with him and make four observations. First, unless education moves beyond reproducing the culture of the new capitalism, it will be unable to act as a transformative social force. Second, the governance of education systems in many parts of the world is now more vertically and horizontally fragmented. National and sub-national governments are joined by international organisations as well as for profit actors in the coordination of education services. This presents new challenges for teachers in schools as to how to overcome fragmentation in the governing of education systems, with different actors promoting their own branded solutions. Third, if it is pedagogy that connects the apparently self-contained act of teaching with culture, structure and mechanism of social control, encompassing the performance of teaching together with the theories, beliefs, policies and controversies that inform and shape it, then we need to bring new pedagogic practices into the classroom as part of the solution (Alexander, 2008). Finally, assessment practices in this area need to move away from high stakes, one size fits all items, to being formative, diagnostic and non-competitive.

However, a series of challenges to the proposal above can immediately be anticipated. One is that the contexts in which many of the key actors discussing the role of education in promoting global competences or global citizenship are in themselves fragmented. For example, looking horizontally across the

UNESCO programmes, it is clear that UNESCO's work suffers from operating in programme silos. Education and culture are placed in separate portfolios, each with their own lines of responsibility, actions and publications. That they do not communicate across the portfolios is evident from their reference lists informing key publications on the need to think with a global outlook. If education is to be the vehicle and institution through which culture is to be acquired – as a way of being, knowing and relating to others – as UNESCO's (2011) report insists, then the different actors involved in governing the education system have much to learn from the other.

The global at the level of the local

Taking the vertical scale and horizontal scales together, global learning can be seen on national and subnational policy agendas across a range of countries. These mappings show a great deal of diversity both within and across national settings reflecting very different ways of framing the key concepts. Bourn et al. (2016) point out that though global learning and sustainability have been on the education agenda for the past ten years, it has been largely left to schools to determine what they might do and how, though typically with few resources.

Bourn et al. (2016) also report a diverse set of agendas to which 'global learning' is a solution. These range from shoring up national identity in the face of other identity claims (e.g. the Fundamental British Values initiative in relation to the rise of Islamic radicalism) to addressing radicalisation leading to global terrorism (such as PREVENT), recognising diversity in classrooms, as a response to the Sustainable Development Goals, and as part of an economic imperative so as to promote global competitiveness. In essence, global learning in the UK has diverse cultural, political and economic objectives, including reinforcing national identities.

Education in classrooms is, by definition, a locally situated affair, though the curriculum, mode of assessment and student body in schools can vary. Examples include international schools for mobile elites, the International Baccalaureate, which is a curriculum and credential which cuts across national boundaries, or the United World Colleges (Reimers, 2013). We can add on here private elite education systems who service the upper/ruling classes within and across national boundaries.

Education has increasingly been subject to global governing, as intergovernmental and multilateral organisations have sought to direct education in national and subnational settings. As we show in the following section, the OECD in particular has mastered governing through an expanding portfolio of indicators and statistics. Their latest foray into global competences is a case in point.

The global as approached by OECD

In 2018, the OECD added measuring global competences to its flagship large-scale assessment tool – the Program of International Student Achievement (PISA). According to the OECD, global competences are needed in young people to enable them to participate in a "more interconnected world but also appreciate and benefit from cultural differences" (OECD, 2018, p. 4). Like UNESCO, the OECD acknowledges societies have become increasingly divided between a small number of those who have benefitted from globalisation, and those whose lives and futures are now increasingly more uncertain and precarious.

Its 2016 *Global Competency for an Inclusive World* and its 2018 *Global Competence Framework* provide us with an insight into how the OECD read the world. For example, a globally competent student in the 2018 Framework Report is one who learns to live harmoniously in multicultural communities, is able to thrive in changing labour markets, able to use media platforms responsibly and supports the realisation of the SDGs. In other words, global competences are:

> a multidimensional capacity. Globally-competent individuals can examine local, global and intercultural issues, understand and appreciate different perspectives and worldviews, interact successfully and respectfully with others, and take responsible action toward sustainability and collective well-being.
>
> *(OECD, 2018:4)*

Evaluating global competences means measuring them so as to provide system level data to countries. This would enable a country's education system to develop interventions that "invite young people to understand the world beyond their immediate environment, interact with others with respect and dignity, and take actions toward building sustainable and thriving communities" (OECD, 2018, pp. 5–6).

These competences draw from a particular framing of global issues, so that as a construct they are difficult to measure across settings. Many of the items on the test are highly complex (cause of poverty). Nevertheless, the OECD PISA test invites responses that range over a continuum from "I have never heard of this" to "I am familiar with this and would be able to explain it well". Items such as inviting students to "discuss the different reasons why people become refugees" could easily result in a pooling of ignorance rather than being a measure of any authentic competence.

There are other problems facing the OECD's global competence project. In 2018, some 30 countries (40% of PISA member countries) declined to administer the test due to the problematic nature of the items, which they argue require deep cultural and contextual knowledge to inform answers. As a result, the items on the test have been limited to cognitive constructs and not beliefs and values. The OECD also has to presume students are familiar with issues that cut across local and national boundaries. Yet even discussions of climate change, or the causes of mass migration, can vary, dependent upon place, politics and the media.

Finally, the OECD's items appear to be underpinned by western values and outlooks which are seen as being imposed on other countries with rather different views of the world. This, in turn, undermines the very premises that drive the test in the first place; of being open to diversity and to the intercultural.

The global as approached by UNESCO

Another set of programmes and initiatives which now are promoting cultural knowledge and skills to secure global understanding comes from UNESCO, who currently play a key role in delivering on the Sustainable Development Goal 4 (education), and Target 4.7 – global citizenship education and sustainability. UNESCO points out there is no agreed definition of global citizenship. However, it goes on to suggest that "there is sufficient consensus on the key principles ... a sense of belonging to the global community, a common humanity and thereby a sense of community toward global wellbeing. This means that global citizenship responsibilities apply to everyone" (2018b, p. 2). It goes on to argue that the globally competent citizen at the heart of Global Citizenship Education (GCED) has the skills to bridge the cultural and social diversity in the world, to examine societal orders and policies, and to make informed choices so as to transform their communities and societies toward being more peaceful, just and sustainable (p. 14). The report also notes that what is needed for GCED to be effective are new approaches supported by serious design, research and evaluation.

In *Preparing Teachers for Global Citizenship Education*, UNESCO (2018b) provide a template for teachers to help inform 'the art of teaching' global citizenship education. Their template is quite open and not prescriptive, though the main areas of knowledge to be addressed are clear: globalisation and interdependence, social justice and inequality, identity and diversity, sustainable development, and peace and conflict (p. 29). It is also directed at teachers who they see as lacking capacity regarding implementing GCED. The template is, in effect, a set of resources to be used by teachers as part of a whole school approach or as part of existing subject lines. In relation to what kind of pedagogy to be engaged in teaching GCED, UNESCO (2018b) argue that what is needed is an approach that goes beyond a cognitive (know that) dimension, to include "actual experiences and opportunities to develop, test and build their own views and attitudes, and to design how to take actions responsibly for the socio-emotional and behavioural dimensions" (p. 19–20).

In 2018, UNESCO (2018c) published a new development in their thinking related to GCED and how they might engage with diverse local realities around the world around deeper civilisational values. The report opts for the term cosmonogy rather than cosmology. Technically, the term 'cosmonogy' refers to the study of the origin of the cosmos itself, or the universe (e.g. big bang theory), which is a more limited idea. This can be contrasted with cosmology, which refers to the study of the universe in its fullest of senses, including its dynamics, evolution and future. It then opts to use the idea of liberty, equality and fraternity (French Republican thinking) to search for equivalences in "local cosmogonies, founding stories and national histories" (UNESCO, 2018c: 2), and in constitutions, national anthems, government policy documents and the writings of historical figures (OECD 2018c: 2). Examples (from 10 in all) from the report include 'ubuntu' (South Africa) – 'I am because we are: we are because I am'; the idea of 'shura' (Oman) – 'consultation'; and 'buen vivir' (Boliviar) – 'living well'. In doing so, it marks an important shift in thinking about the cultural within the context of the global as more than how well individuals relate to each other, and their capacity to participate in a community. Its search for equivalences to a European world view, however, imposes an important limit on the range of other cultures and their cosmologies (e.g. indigenous New Zealanders) who presumably are not valued as they are different rather than equivalent.

The global and culture

In light of the previous discussion, we note that both the OECD and UNESCO point to the important role of culture in mediating the global. But what do they mean when they talk about culture, for there is no one single definition or conceptualisation? The literature broadly identifies culture as working at several levels; at the level of the individual (meaning making); a community or communities to which an individual belongs (social bonds) and at the level of a society (worldviews), or societies, as in diasporic communities (c.f. Cox and Schechter, 2002).

Too individual a focus on culture, for example, an individual's understanding of an issue is dogged by methodological individualism. By way of contrast, assuming that everyone in any particular society holds the same view is a case of stereotyping. In any one society, there are degrees of diversity as a result of our capacity to reflect critically on what we see around us. This doesn't, or shouldn't, mean seeing culture everywhere, but rather we take 'culture' as a starting point and question those assumptions that are likely to determine how we account for degrees of diversity. Through critical reflection we can make more visible to ourselves the structuring assumptions about worldmaking in a bigger societal, or cosmological, sense, and in doing so expand our horizons of understanding and actions.

So where does this leave us, and what does this mean for a classroom teacher? First, we agree with UNESCO (2011), who state we need to go beyond acknowledging the "fruitful diversity of cultures" within a national context. When UNESCO call for the embrace of "cultural diversity" in a global context, this ought to enable us to place the individual in potentially multiple communities and societies, which includes, but is not limited to, the national context to which they were born or are a passport holder for. Cultural diversity in a global context implies not only other (societal or cosmological) ways in which individuals and communities see the world in comparison to one's own, but an openness to the other, along with a willingness to challenge one's own cultural horizons.

Second, approaching culture as a dynamic process implies moving beyond essentialist understandings, such as those that associate it with a country or language. A non-essentialist view acknowledges cultures as dynamic, which cuts across national frontiers as communities expand and extend beyond the boundaries of nation states to even include online communities.

Third, understanding culture at a societal level means recognising the structuring effects of different civilisations (Cox and Schechter, 2002). Civilisation, Cox notes, is especially relevant in understanding global change today. We often don't talk about culture at this level – in part because it is so much part of the taken for granted common sense of a shared reality. Yet, Cox's three dimensions of time/space, individuality/community and spirituality/cosmogony, and his discussion, is a fruitful line for inquiry in our approach to cultural diversity, and the complexities to be accounted for so as to move towards 'global' understanding.

Across different civilisations, notions of time and space, the tensions between individual and community, and finally notions of spirituality that carry and convey the relationship between nature and the cosmos, shape very different realities, and thus common-sense understandings. And it is precisely these realities that are culturally shaped, and with which we as humans operate in and on the world. By reflecting on these dimensions, we can take steps to enable us to recognize "there are different perspectives on the world, different understandings about the nature of the world, different perceptions of reality" (Cox and Schecter, 2002, p. 163).

Notions of *time and space* might be a valuable starting point in any classroom reflection on cultural diversity within the global. How are teachers grappling with two dimensions? Do our pedagogic practices take into account these dimensions, and the significance they might have for students' culturally diverse representations and identifications? Understanding the multiplicities of distinct perspectives of time and space is essential, if we are to orient our minds towards more inclusive pedagogic practices. This means not only acknowledging the cultural diversity we meet in our classrooms, but recognising it, and respecting it as it comes to us.

Equally valuable is a second dimension of difference between civilisation – *the tensions between the individual and the community*, which Cox does not see as "mutually exclusive categories", but rather as sitting in different relations of priority in different world societies. When some societies place the individual before the community, or vice versa, what issues are present, and what problems are overcome? At the core of this tension is how we move from seeing when and why an 'individualistic' orientation is useful and when a collective one is important. When is too much individualism an issue in the context of societal and global challenges? Equally important, it is necessary to ask, when do we need to work together as a community to resolve problems? Surely those problems facing us at the present, including the challenges of climate change, are one such occasion. How are we, then, as educators, to think the global in terms of these tensions, and how might the global be a resource to think and act differently?

A third dimension in understanding culture as civilisation is 'the common notion of the relationship of humanity to nature and the cosmos", or spirituality or cosmology" (Cox and Schechter, 2002, p. 177) brings into view fundamental assumptions about the nature of the world and of humanity's place in it, "having expressions in conflicts concerning material life – in the connections of race, gender, ethnicity and religion with economic oppression, and in the common fate of humanity in fragile biosphere" (2002, p. 178).

UNESCO's move in the direction of a civilisational approach, with 'cosmonogy', is suggestive of a wider understanding of culture. However, UNESCO needs to move away from a big bang equivalent account of how the world began to a cosmological approach. In doing so, they should be encouraged to go beyond analogues of western enlightenment ideas. Instead, they should explore both similarities and differences in diverse cosmologies, and how these – together – might be resources for engaging with global challenges. Rather than being oblivious to the multiple forms and ways in which humans represent themselves across centuries, we would rather acknowledge them in understanding 'a global' that recognises and brings into dialogue their manifestations, and in doing so, aim towards a better understanding of our complex, diverse, humanity and our relationship to nature, the planet and each other.

A dialogic approach

Quite rightly, a teacher is justified in prodding us to be more concrete regarding what they might do in their classrooms. Our first comment is that as a professionally trained pedagogue, teachers need to be attuned to the fact that each decision about what and how to teach is a decision guided by values (what is important, and to whom) and theories (why this concept now, where does it come from, etc.?). To not acknowledge this is to think technocratically about life in classrooms. All knowledge is political, as the feminists remind us, and knowledge/power is intimately linked.

As a starting point, we suggest that teachers insist that global competence tests are an anathema to thinking globally. Instead, they might move through a series of steps, meant to generate conversations, and create new knowledges and understanding in the classroom (see Figure 7.1). These steps are not in any obligatory order. Each step moves outward from the individual to the wider communities and societies, but each step can also be an entry point in engaging in classroom dialogue.

Step one asks: what does it mean to be a global citizen at the level of the person? What obligations and responsibilities does it imply? What common problems are shared, and how might individuals stimulate conversations that help overcome these issues? Where there are differences, what are the causes of these differences, as we perceive them? What role do different perspectives, experiences, access to resources, aspirations for the future, mean for coming to also understand the other?

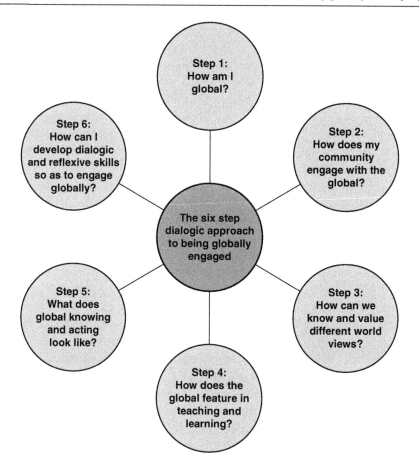

Figure 7.1 A Six Step Dialogic Approach to Knowing About and Acting Globally

Step two asks: what does belonging to a community imply for an individual and their responsibilities when addressing global issues? Do all communities the individual belongs to see the issues in the same way? If not, why not, and what are the cultural, political and economic reasons for this? What about communities the individual does not belong to? Or those from which they have been forced to leave? How might they speak over divides to arrive at an understanding that recognises differences and similarities? Are communities mediated by technologies (such as online communities) similar to, or different from, those that take place without digital technologies? What responsibilities and obligations to each other operate in a digitally mediated community world?

Step three asks: what are the implications of different world views, and the common-sense understandings that these worldviews generate, for how we engage with each other, and with common global issues? Do those societies with world views which privilege individualism over collectivism face

107

particular challenges around coming together when a collective response is needed? What can they learn from those societies whose world views promote collective interests over the individual in order to resolve global challenges, and vice versa?

Step four asks: what curriculum, pedagogies and modes of assessment might be deployed in the classroom? How might these modes promote an active role for learners as knowledge creators? What might a curriculum based on the global challenges facing individuals, communities and societies look like? Which forms of assessment encourage reflexivity and exploratory work, and are attuned to personal and interpersonal transformation? UNESCO has provided a useful list of resources teachers might access to help direct activities in classrooms. However, these are resources to stimulate more open dialogical approaches, and are to be added to as a global reservoir of knowledges that can be used to think about the process of globalisation itself, its trends, scenarios, challenges and opportunities, and what young learners themselves can and will do to mediate these issues.

Step five asks: what does successful acquisition of a global perspective look like? Can students recognise these attributes? Is there a continuum of improvement, or a back and forth movement, as new problems and challenges are encountered? Do the developmental levels of students matter for what is engaged with when in the classroom?

Step six asks: how can dialogue, reflexivity and discussions around values be fostered in the classroom so as to enable students to acquire the attributes to become globally aware? This will require more than monologic reflections. Potential contributions to further our knowledges will not happen outside dialogue. For it is only through dialogue that these can be made visible, known to students, and worked out. In promoting dialogue as a pedagogical approach in the classroom, it means placing on the table those knowledges, skills and values that will enable young people to recognise, reflect, adjudicate and transform their understandings of the world.

Dialogue and reflexivity, listening and learning, are key skills here. We support Alexander's view, that: "dialogue about education is a prerequisite for social and economic progress. Dialogue within the classroom lays the foundations not just of successful learning, but also of social cohesion, active citizenship and the good society" (2008, p. 122). By dialogue, Alexander does not mean a mere conversation that "people reductively call communication skills", or to what characterises a political dialogue, empty of content value but described as 'constructive' (p. 122). It is rather a dialogue that "requires willingness and skill to engage with minds, ideas and ways of thinking other than our own" (op. cit). This requires openness to listening, and adopting a critical, reflexive approach to one's teaching by taking into consideration children's ideas and ideals, and how they can become makers of futures.

By way of a conclusion

It is clear that the kinds of questions above to shape dialogues and practices in schools are antithetical to global testing, as we see with the OECD's PISA Global Competence Framework, with its focus on a right cognitive answer. Being globally competent does not mean knowing the right answer. Rather, it sits on the other side of the question/answer divide by privileging asking critical, reflexive questions and then exploring differences in responses as well as similarities. It also means being attentive to the affective dimension of learners and learning; of how we feel about things, others, ourselves and why these matter for what we in the end choose to do. Being globally competent means being able to appreciate and interrogate multiple dimensions of the cultural – from the individual to the community and society, and to work with both similarity and difference.

If we get it right in the classroom, argues Reimers, learners will begin to develop the capacity "to do, to create and to innovate in addressing shared global challenges" (2013, p. 61). We agree with Reimers. What is needed is the active and reflexive development in students of those knowledges, values and skills which might transform the world and its global challenges. This means exploring and putting into practice the kind of cosmological understanding, like 'compassion' for neighbours and nature, that means actions toward the other, nature, and the planetary change.

References

Alexander, R. (2008) *Essays in Pedagogy*, London: Routledge.

Bourn, D., Hunt, F., Blum, N. and Lawson, H. (2016) *Primary Education for Global Learning and Sustainability, Research Report*, Cambridge: Cambridge Primary Review Trust.

Boven, M. and Wille, A. (2017) *Diploma Democracy: The Rise of Political Meritocracy*, Oxford: Oxford University Press.

Cohen, J. (2019) Populism and the Politics of Resentment. In: *Jus Cogen: A Critical Journal of the Philosophy of Law and Politics*.

Cox, R. W. and Schechter, M. (2002) *The Political Economy of a Plural World: Critical Reflections on Power, Morals and Civilization*, London: Routledge.

IPCC (2014) *Climate Change 2014: Synthesis Report Summary for Policymakers*, Geneva: IPCC.

Mittelman, J. H. (2004) *Whither Globalisation? The Vortex of Knowledge and Economy*, London: Routledge.

OECD (2008) *Growing Unequal?*, Paris: OECD.

OECD (2011) *Divided We Stand: Why Inequality Keeps on Rising*, Paris: OECD.

OECD (2018) *PISA: Preparing Our Youth for an Inclusive and Sustainable World. The OECD Global Competence Framework*, Paris: OECD.

Piketty, T. (2014) *Capital in the Twenty-First Century*, Cambridge: Harvard University Press.

Reimers, F. (2013) Education for Improvement: Citizenship in the Global Public Sphere. *Harvard International Review*, 35(1), 56–61.

Sennett, R. (2006) *The Culture of the New Capitalism*, New Haven, CT: Yale University Press.

UNESCO (2011) *A New Cultural Policy Agenda for Development and Mutual Understanding: Key Arguments for a Strong Commitment to Cultural Diversity and Intercultural Dialogue*, Paris: UNESCO.

UNESCO (2018a) *Preventing Violent Extremism Through Education: Effective Activities and Impact*, Paris: UNESCO.

UNESCO (2018b). *Preparing Teachers for Global Citizenship Education. A Template*, Bangkok: UNESCO Asia and Pacific Regional Bureau for Education.

UNESCO (2018c) *Global Citizenship Education: Taking it Local*, Paris: UNESCO.

8

Education as the embracing of a loving universe
Designing an inclusive curriculum

Graham Schweig and Nitesh Gor

Introduction

Using the word 'Love' in educational contexts is not commonplace in UK education. Defining the aims and purpose of education as one that considers the nature of the soul and the enactment of the soul through life is also uncommon territory. And yet, for the Avanti schools, it is central to the vision and design of the ethos and curriculum. Love, as a universal human need and the right to love, as a human right, makes us what we are, who we are, how we are and for the spiritual philosophical principles upon which we design our curriculum and educational experience for our children, *why* we are. From the perspective of ancient Hindu sacred literature (Vedic), Love *is* the Divine, it is the source of all that exists and is unlimited. And so, through philosophical enquiry and opportunities to experience Love, we developed a curriculum that aimed to be inclusive and which would develop the child in holistic ways.

There is another principle upon which our curriculum is designed: that education is a relational activity. Referring to Gergen's theory of the *relational being* (Gergen, 2009), our aims concur with the suggestion that education is a set of processes intended to *enhance relationships*. As well as achieving educational excellence, our aim is to develop, in our children and community, an awareness of their relationships with self (the nature of the soul or spirit), with family, with truth, with justice, with society, with community, with the natural world and essentially, a unique loving relationship with the Divine. This interest in relational schools can be seen in the work of Professor Robert Coe (https://relationalschools.org/resources/). We understood, however, that it is a radical departure from most mainstream educational research and practice, which is designed to enhance solely the individual's mind.

In this chapter, we introduce the conception of Avanti Schools as the first designated Hindu state schools in the United Kingdom. We then describe the principles upon which we have designed our curriculum, linking the Vedic scriptural guidance with contemporary research about dialogue, before giving examples of the ways that our philosophy of religious and ethics curriculum is lived out in our various schools. We explain a set of values that guide our decision making and refer to the literature that suggests that a significant ethical development of our time is the recovery of ancient wisdom about the importance of character: "We need good character to lead ethical, productive, and fulfilling lives. We need good character to create a just, compassionate, and productive society" (Lickona, 2015: p. 4).

A beginning

Avanti Schools Trust was conceived in 2003 with a vision to establish the first state-funded Hindu faith schools in England. Our first school opened in 2008 as a single form entry primary school in Harrow. We understand that there is contestation about the very existence of state-funded faith schools. There is often misrepresentation about what these schools do, and in particular for the unusual existence of Hindu-faith schools, and how they prepare young people for modern socially complex life in the 21st century. How can a tradition that is over 5,000 years old serve children who will retire in about 2080? Whilst our purpose was initially focused on providing the opportunity for families to choose an 'Eastern' Hindu-based education, we also wanted the schools to be fully inclusive and welcoming of all faiths and to those who had none. How could this possibly be? How could one religious tradition create an educational experience that was rooted in the Vedic principles yet also truly open to the diverse communities we hoped to serve? From early on, it was clear to us that the tension between inclusivity and fidelity needed to be resolved if we were to offer something meaningful in our education provision.

To begin, we needed to be clear about the purpose of education. We sought early inspiration from Vedic scriptures: a line of the Srimad Bhagavatam (one of Hinduism's most important texts) teaching: "the highest truth is reality distinguished from illusion for the welfare of all". The purpose of education had to be more than just academic knowledge, it had to also contribute to wellbeing – and not just of the individual, but for all of society.

The Avanti vision (version 2019)

Why we're here...

Avanti exists to help each person become a well-rounded human being through intellectual, moral and spiritual growth, and so make the world a better place.

Our core principles...

- We are unique spiritual beings with incredible potential and we achieve our full potential by discovering and nurturing all parts of ourselves — intellectual, emotional, physical and spiritual.
- We choose how we wish to respond to life and what we nurture within us.
- We care for and respect all life — human, animal and plant — and live in a way that causes the least possible harm.
- We each observe the one same reality from our own unique perspective and engage in open-minded dialogue to deeply enrich our vision.
- We serve a higher purpose by living a meaningful and satisfying life of contribution.
- We are nourished by personal relationships that fulfil our need to love and be loved, encouraging us to be the best we can be.

From this starting point, we developed what would became the three key pillars of our vision: educational excellence, character formation and spiritual insight. The words ('educational' and not 'academic', 'formation' and not 'development', 'spiritual insight' and not one of a number of other possible descriptions) were specifically chosen to highlight our desire for a holistic, reflexive and inclusive form of education. Many of these principles chimed with the findings of the Cambridge Primary Review, including a focus on academic performance as well as spiritual, moral, cultural, mental and physical development.

As well as the three guiding tenets of education excellence, character formation and spiritual insight, we agreed upon six key values for our curriculum design: empathy, respect, self-discipline, courage, gratitude and integrity. The theological belief in values-education was affirmed by the research base that, "The research evidence is clear: schools that are values-driven have high expectations and demonstrate academic, professional and social success" (Arthur et al., 2015: p. 9).

Since Avanti Schools Trust opened the first state-funded Hindu school in 2008, there was of course no pre-existing religious studies (RS) curriculum which we could draw from, at least none that drew its inspiration from Hinduism. As our schools grew, the curriculum design principles and implementation became in competition with the practical, operational efforts of opening and building schools. Nevertheless, as our capacity grew, a small team began work on what we would call our Philosophy, Religion & Ethics curriculum (PRE). One of the first things we had to understand were the theological principles that should underpin such a curriculum and to do so we asked two questions: what is the theological vision? How do we want our young people to be when they leave our schools? And the perennial question: how would it be an inclusive curriculum that acknowledged diversity of belief, with or without religious faith?

Theological vision and principles

The key educational principles on which the Avanti Schools rest are drawn from carefully selected philosophical tenets found in the timeless narratives, teachings and wisdom of the Vedic, Vedāntic and Purāṇic literature of India; the core sacred texts of Hindu religions. In the oldest sacred texts of the world, we find the still applicable and exigent principle of dialogue:

ekaṃ sad viprā bahudhā vadanti

There is one (*ekaṃ*) Reality (*sad*)
about which vibrant persons (*viprā*)
in various ways (*bahudhā*) speak (*vadanti*).

(Rig Veda 1.164.46)

And the following ancient parable shows how humans can share in dialogue what they experience and what they perceive. There is a well-known story about six blind people and an elephant that illustrates the Rig Veda sense of multiple versions of the truth – and the importance of speaking and listening as key pedagogic principles.

One day, six blind people were walking along a path when they came across an obstruction. "What is this?" they said. Each person stretched their hands out and felt the object: it is a fan, a dagger, a tree trunk, a wall, a snake, a rope. Each description was incomplete. So, confused, they sat together and talked about their experience of touching the obstruction: eventually, through the discussion, they realised that they had come across an elephant.

Such dialogic switches in perspective (Phillipson and Wegerif, 2017), listening to other people's ideas, speaking one's own ideas and bridging the gaps that exist between different ideas, symbolised important learning characteristics that we wished to nurture throughout our curriculum. Therefore, children need plentiful opportunities for dialogue about invariant concepts so that they could hold broad and multiple perspectives on common realities.

If dialogue was to be a key feature of our curriculum, we needed to be explicit about the nature of the one reality about which 'deeply inspired people speak' – how would our children gain knowledge and insights into complex philosophical concepts (like 'who am I?' or 'What is the purpose of life?') and then engage in dialogue about them? Again, we turned to the scriptural guidance, knowing that the essential and elaborately illuminated principle drawn from these literatures and sources, which became foundational for Avanti schools, is the simple but deeply nuanced principle of Love. Indeed, Love is both the most powerful striving in humans and Love is also the powerful principle in the theologies of Hindu traditions (as it is for many religions). It is a principle that transcends the distinction between the secular and the sacred, and that is how Avanti can coherently lead both non-traditional, non-denominational schools alongside denominational, Hindu faith-based schools.

The principle of Love is about embracing reality. Reality already embraces us from without, from within and from all around us. Avanti education is about learning to appreciate this deeply, more and more, and how we can more and more return the embrace of Reality. What does this mean for our children and the teachers who teach them? What is reality? How do we bring children to an awareness of their own reality (given their developmental stages) and how do we develop their understanding of Love as the Divine, in ways that are meaningful, inclusive and not indoctrination? It was important that children and teachers be given opportunities to explore how to embrace life, embrace the world, the universe and all of reality. An *embrace* is about, on the one hand, a total appreciation and acceptance of the way things are, with a knowledge of the way things are. It is about genuine understanding, genuine inquiry and selfless attention given the phenomena. On the other hand, an *embrace* is about a passion to enter the mystery of these phenomena and how they beckon children to go further and further into a closer and closer relationship with reality.

Building on this, we understood the principle of Love to be about relationships. This is consistent with the academic literature about the socio-emotional benefits for pupils of schools taking a relational approach (Gergen, 2009), in particular, the central importance of the relationship between educator and learner (Brunerm, 1996). Education is not merely a teacher's presentation to students of the knowledge of this or that discipline, though certainly that is part of it. Education, and the business of teaching, involves (1) *agency*, taking control of one's mental activity. (2) Developing the ability to *reflect* – to make sense of learning through discussion. (3) Being in a community of learners, what the Hindu tradition would call *sanga* and through *collaboration* to share the resources of the mix of humans being involved in teaching and learning. And (4), consider diverse ways of life, or *culture*, and how we construct, negotiate, institutionalise and settle on our sense of reality (Brunerm, 1996: p. 87). Paulo Freire (2005) argued that knowledge is a process of co-construction, involving, in essence, a conversation that opens possibility thinking and what Greene (1998) calls a social imagination: together, in dialogue that involves argumentation, critique and experience, new ways of engaging in or embracing the world can be developed. This is also strongly evident in social constructivist psychological theories of learning, particularly the work of Russian psychologist Vygotsky. As well as the absorption of the knowledge from this or that discipline, we emphasised the more subtle task within the experienced curriculum, one of cultivating a *relationship* of the learner to that discipline. A relationship in which the learner finds ways of embracing his or her world with greater curiosity and inspiration, with more sensitivity and caring, with ultimately more of a desire to delve more deeply into this relationship and the very nature of things. As a learner moves through an Avanti education, as well as a growing passion for knowledge, there is an aspiration that so too will they experience a real sense of *humility* before the wondrous existence in which they find themselves.

If we consider that Love is about embracing the opportunities in life, through learning, and that this is fostered through high-quality relationships, it is a natural extension that dialogue is the vehicle through which greater awareness is developed. In the Hindu tradition, the principle of Love is about the three well-balanced components of dialogue. First, it is about the humble receptivity of hearing, of listening, of openness and attentiveness, and suspending judgement. Second, it is also about making a contribution, offering speech that passionately asserts and expresses a commitment, a vision and perspective. And then finally, both interlocutors in dialogue experience, ideally, a balance of reciprocation and playful movement between the listening and speaking roles that lifts both listener and speaker to a new elevated state of community and a greater sense of reality. It is this kind of dialogue that is sought and cultivated in the Avanti approach to education and is evident also in the academic literature (see Coltman and Rolls' chapter in this book).

Dialogue as revelation – as revealing something about oneself, one's family or friendships, community, society, ways of thinking and being, and for those with a faith, one's relationship with the Divine was an important quality of the ways in which we wanted to learn. What this means in an education context is that the first assumption is that there is a constructed space for a dialogue. This is informed by strong and respectful relationships. Everyone should know that no one will be ridiculed for having an idea and sharing it. Our space for dialogue inculcated our values of empathy, respect, integrity, gratitude, courage and self-discipline. The second point is that we each strive to construct a relationship with the One Reality (which in the Hindu tradition of Avanti is the total sum of Krishna, His energies and the spiritual self – Sri Bhajana-rahasya by Srila Bhaktivinode Thakura, chapter 2). We each live through a particular *way of life*, which influences how we think, how we are, how and what we believe and how we make sense of the world, both material and spiritual within and around us. It is through discussion or dialogue with another person (who is experiencing their own striving for a relationship with the One Reality) that a greater awareness of the One Reality is revealed: this is social construction of knowledge. Furthermore, a deeper appreciation of the human community as a conduit between the human and reality could be cultivated. Importantly, and drawing from Gert Biesta's thinking, beyond teaching children's useful knowledge and behaving in socially acceptable ways, the third (and for Avanti a key aspect) is to enable children to come to be independent people with a voice of their own, able to think for themselves and to take real responsibility for their decisions and for other people (see Phillipson and Wegerif, 2017, and Wegerif, 2010, for greater discussion). For us, this is in relation to the universal human feeling of Love and from a theological position, that Love is the manifestation of the Divine or Krishna.

How can two people, with different beliefs and practising different religions or none, develop their relationship with one another, through listening from each other, and through this listening, deepening their own appreciation of their own belief system? Here is a conversation retold from a first-hand perspective that illustrates the point.

Dialogue between senior member of Hindu community (SM) and new headteacher to Avanti (HT)

HT: So, I understand that from your view, that the spirit is the self. I have also looked at this from a view that we are all energy.

SM: I like that idea. I would add that I don't see it as an "impersonal" energy. The Bhagavad-gita speaks about all living beings as eternal spiritual sparks, who are the energy of God. And that God is also an individual person.

HT: I've also thought about it from the perspective of material energy. What do you think about the idea that we are essentially material energy, not spiritual?

SM: I struggle with that concept for a few reasons. It would call into question freewill – chemicals don't have freewill. If we are "material" energy, and when we die we get "recycled" into the universe, then perhaps it doesn't matter what we do here on earth? Is that how you think of that?

HT: So, you would refer to karmic reaction in that case? So, if I kill something it will be added to my karma and I would pay for it later on in this life?

SM: This life or the next life! The concept of karma combines both a sense of destiny (we are not always in control of the circumstances we find ourselves in) and of agency (we can choose how we respond to that circumstance.)

HT: I like the concept of karma. It can be quite difficult to explain it, especially as it can be seen as judgmental.

SM: Yes, I would agree. I like the way the Bhagavad-gita explains it. We may perceive someone being in a relatively worse off condition than ourselves. One view could be to feel a sense of superiority. But firstly, karma implies that we could just as easily be in a worse position ourselves tomorrow, or in a past or future life – so there is no place for hubris. And secondly, we are not judging that other person's mental state or even their character – all of which might be more evolved than our own.

HT: So, if I eat a fish, my "karma" is affected, because I have caused the death of a creature. But surely that is different, because we know that fish omega 3 oils are beneficial for us. Fish oil is good?

SM: Well, it is not so good for the fish.

In the conversation, statements and counter statements were made, followed up by questions and examples to illustrate the points they were each trying to make. The tone is respectful. The opportunity to learn together is evident. So, whether the Headteacher perhaps continued to eat fish because it was good for him or not, the conversation would have deepened awareness of the issues of meat eating as related to self and the notion of spirit. It also connected the day to day practice of eating with a moral purpose of conserving life. The point is that through dialogue, deeper relationship making is made with greater sense creation. Referring to Bruner's four qualities of teaching and learning, the conversation above evidences agency of thought, reflection in posing questions and deliberating and the learning of cultural ways of life that each brought to the conversation. Dialogue is also about change and not necessarily sticking to one position. The Headteacher became a vegetarian, mindful that it was not good for the fish!

The principle of Love is about what is innermost in relation to everything else: how do we develop Loving relationships in all we do? Thus, what we tried to do is to attain the true spirit of the original meaning of the word *education* itself—'to educate' in the word's original Latin, *educere*, means 'to lead out' or 'to bring out'. Our curriculum philosophy believes that each student possesses within his or her deeper self the resources for greater insights and original contributions. The very personal approach, therefore, is committed to and involves engaging both the 'inner teacher' as well as the 'outer teacher' in the pursuit of knowledge. The inner teacher draws from the affective and intuitive faculties of the student along with the outer teacher who nourishes the cognitive and interactive faculties. In many ways, the approach is a very tangible, holistic one. It requires the teacher also to be open, humble and willing to engage in meaningful dialogue that truly deepens children's knowledge, understanding and experiences of the One Reality or Divine.

The concepts are complex and, at first, we struggled to translate these ancient principles into a 21st century context, even though intuitively and philosophically they were as robust and relevant as ever. A number of questions remained: how would we present these theological concepts and philosophical ideas for primary aged children? How would teachers need to adapt their pedagogies to create spaces for dialogue in a UK National curriculum that is already saturated and knowledge-laden? And most importantly, how do we want our young people to be?

A vision for the future: how do we want our young people to be?

Having established our purpose and vision for education, and the underpinning theological principles, further questions arose:

- What does this mean for education in the 21st century?
- What pedagogical insights can we glean from ancient scriptures?

- How can teachers and school leaders make sense of this when most haven't experienced the education we are trying to create?
- How do we balance the needs of such a form of education with those required by government and regulatory bodies?

We set out to create a Philosophy Religions Ethics (PRE) curriculum and soon realised that it would need to be far more than that. We needed the curriculum to draw on the pedagogical principles which we wished to see manifest throughout the entire school. We also wanted, in the longer-term, for there to be coherence across all subjects, centred around the big questions of the PRE curriculum across both primary and secondary phases. As we began, we were confronted with similar questions that any curriculum designer might face:

- How do we see progress?
- What is spiritual progress?
- Should this be a linear or spiral curriculum?
- Should we structure the curriculum along the lines of theological concepts? Or do we follow the flow of the key narratives/epics? Or do we structure it along the lines of the key philosophical concepts? Or perhaps the topics of applied ethics?
- How do we ensure appropriate matching of topics to a child's psychological development?
- How will we support teachers, and in particular, with the lack of subject knowledge in Hinduism, to teach and inspire children?
- How do we support leaders to overcome their resistance to something new?
- How do we support professional learning and experience of spiritual development so that it is meaningful for teachers who have to teach children about the soul?

The nature of philosophy, theology and ethics lends itself to adopting a spiral curriculum. You can have a very deep and meaningful conversation about, for example, whether God exists, or why do good people suffer, with a child in Reception as can you with a student in Year 13. Each will be different because language and vocabulary will define the depth of dialogue. It also will be different because knowledge and understanding of the world, and children's experiences of the world will be different between a four-year-old and an eighteen-year-old learner.

During initial planning sessions, we documented how we might assess the effectiveness and impact of our curriculum intentions. As our curriculum involved helping children develop a sense of character (as a relational, ethical, inclusive and loving attitude to the world), we decided to start at the end of their educational journey with us (as a through school we also looked to Year 13). The Jubilee Centre for Character Education also emphasised this point: "Each school needs to describe the kinds of persons it wants to help develop and then outline the philosophy that underlies its approach in the development of its students" (Arthur et al., 2015: p. 9). In our search to develop an inclusive curriculum that was also rooted in our Eastern philosophy, we agreed with the position of the Jubilee centre about what character education was *not*:

- Character education is *not* about promoting the moral ideals of a particular moral system. Rather, it aims to promote a **core set of universally acknowledged cosmopolitan virtues**.
- Character education is **not about moral indoctrination mindless conditioning**. The ultimate goal of all proper character education is to equip students with the intellectual tools to choose wisely of their own accord within the framework of a democratic society. Critical thinking is central to a well-rounded character.
- Character and virtue are *not* essentially religious notions. Almost all current theories of virtue and character education are couched in a post-religious language.

Table 8.1 shows different qualities of thinking, being and knowledge focusing on our six values. For example, if we wanted courage as a character quality, what would this 'look like' at the end of Year 2, Year 4, Year 6 etcetera?

However, whilst this exercise was valuable in drawing together a developmental overview of values, it became necessary to be detailed and specific

Table 8.1 Defining our expectations

Character Area	By the end of Yr2	By the end of Yr4	By the end of Yr6/7
Respect	Demonstrate respectful attitudes to school life through: • Good manners • Sharing • Listening to others before answering Respect their ability to choose Understand that people have different faiths	Demonstrate respectful attitudes (All of previous and...) • Discuss importance of respectful attitudes towards Nature (Yr3) • Learn to disagree respectfully (Yr4) • Explore different relationships in families and society Understand how to display respect to other people (looking at different cultural traditions e.g. gesture)	Demonstrate respectful attitudes through: • Think about their behaviours and how these impact on other people • Justify their viewpoint with increasingly well thought-out arguments • Acknowledge other people's viewpoints whilst disagreeing or holding a different viewpoint • Participate in and know the value of healthy lifestyles (emotionally and physically) • Explore how respect is shown in Vedic texts

about the knowledge content, remembering the principle of dialogue around One Reality.

Building from this, we started organising the curriculum along lines of **philosophical concepts**. We felt that this would help us hook the curriculum onto big questions, and it did. However, a tension emerged in bringing together these with certain ethical or theological concepts. We revised the structure to introduce a mix based around half-termly blocks ensuring that each year had a good balance across philosophy, theology and ethics. Much of Hinduism was traditionally taught through narrative (readers may have heard of the Ramayana or Mahabharata for example), and we wanted to maintain an element of this also. We created a bank of over 150 stories, about half from Hindu scriptures and the other half from other world religions or wisdom tales. We also compiled a reading list that could compliment the curriculum as teaching resources.

The spiral and blended approach to structuring the curriculum helped us address the question about what 'developmentally appropriate' learning was. For example, we could easily match age-related expectations and topic complexity with other national curriculum subjects. What we did find in practice, very interestingly, was that the dialogic nature of the subject meant that students were ready to engage in a topic at a deeper philosophical and ethical level than we had predicted (for example, a Year 3 child learning about Deity worship asked if God was present everywhere, could she worship her pencil). These types of responses from children were a pleasant surprise and spurred us on. Perhaps too, an interesting area for future research.

Another attempt to organise the complex theological and philosophical knowledge content was made because the same question kept arising: What was the knowledge that children needed to be able to discuss and how would we present knowledge about many different philosophical and theological positions? We drew from the work of Rasamandala Das, an eminent scholar and author of comparative religious studies books. In so doing, with Rasamandala, we identified three overarching knowledge bases: (A) foundations and origins (B) spiritual/sacred practices and (C) living in the world. Furthermore, a number of categories evolved (see Table 8.2).

This mapping allowed us greater clarity about the specific forms of knowledge that children could be taught to give them the ability to be 'deeply inspired'. It also invited us to ask questions about what we wanted our children to know and consider how we might teach this knowledge. Without this, what would they engage in dialogue about? In setting out what knowledge and how the values might be experienced, understood and then assessed, we began making explicit links between the theology and philosophy and practice within classrooms. The following two examples of the ways the curriculum design developed are drawn from a Key Stage 3 class and an Early Years' class. The author of the first vignette, Pradip, is a philosopher and theologian and currently the Head of the PRE department at Avanti Fields School (see Box 8.1).

Table 8.2 Avanti Schools Curriculum: mapping knowledge

Main Category	Sub-category	Definition/Deepening thinking
1. History	Date started	Where did each religion start? What is the chronology and how does each religion and/or belief system interconnect in spatial time?
	Place of origin	What geography could be taught to make sense of the space in which particular faith systems started and evolved?
	Founder(s)	What can we learn from the people who 'started' the religion?
		What values could be learnt? How do we teach these?
		How do we inspire interest in autobiography?
		How do children discern which 'important' figure is one in whose footsteps they could follow?
	Symbol(s)	What are the symbols of each religion? How did they come about?
2. Sacred texts	Main divisions	How did religions change over time?
	Key texts	What are the key texts in each religion and how do they interconnect? E.g. do they all have the importance of Love?
3. Teachings	Self	How does each religion understand the notion of self? E.g. as soul?
	Afterlife	What does each religion say about death and what happens after death?
		How do atheists and humanists make sense of the afterlife?
	The world	What does it mean to be on the earth?
	God	How is the Divine understood? Do religions use images/symbols to understand the Divine?
	Term for God	How do religions refer to God?
	Names for God	What names do they use and what do these mean?
	Goal of life	What is the point and meaning of life?
	Other key concepts	Is there anything else that we need to find out about different religions?
	Values	What do religions and religious communities value?
4. Worship and meditation	Practices	How do different religious communities practice?
	Places of worship	Where do different religious communities practice?
	Focus	What is important in a religious place of workship? E.g. facing towards Mecca for Muslims

5. Holy places	Holy sites	Holy sites
	Pilgrimage	Pilgrimage
6. Special times	Festivals	Festivals
	Rites of passage	Rites of passage
	Performing arts	Performing arts
7. Engaging in the modern world	Topical issues and concerns	How do religious beliefs have synergy with modern secular beliefs or liberalism?
		How do young people navigate between religious faith and principles and the diverse diversities in contemporary life?

Box 8.1: Vignette by Pradip Gajjar, head of PRE at Avanti Fields School

The PRE curriculum has a strong knowledge base. It shapes and moulds challenging concepts taught in ancient scripture with opportunity for questioning, debate and appreciation of its application in modern life. It is this opportunity, implicit and central to the curriculum, which drives how it is taught. From lesson to lesson though, the flow may not always be smooth and changes as well as reflective adjustments allow for better connection with the students. It was during a module on the Self, which asked the question 'Who am I?' We started by exploring Plato's chariot analogy and the Bhagavad Gita's car and driver analogy. We then added role play to this:

> "So, (throwing my car keys to a student) there's my car with a full tank of petrol, it has the best alloys – but is it currently going anywhere?"
> " No!"
> " Well, you have the keys. What do you need to do next?"
> "Ok, I need to get into the car and then I can drive it?"

The experience of driving is still theoretical, for most students, and so the idea of the self (the driver) being different or distinct to the body or mind remained an ethereal concept. The philosophical grasp of distinctiveness – of self (or spirit) and body – remained a challenge. I then introduced the idea of discrimination, however, and things started to change. The students devoured the news articles I shared with a passionate awakening of justice. Their contestation shuddered through the classroom as they made connections with stories they had heard on the news and things that mattered to them personally.

"How can someone drag a Sikh student from the bar because of his head gear?"

"What do you mean women have only been allowed to vote in the last 100 years? Why couldn't they have their own bank account or buy their own house?"

"Who says black and Asian doctors should get paid £10,000 less than the white doctors?"

"Is it right to say a Hindu chaplain has a low birth?"

"Aren't we all equal, the same?"

I believe we had hit a philosophical hot button – connecting ancient concepts with modern realities of social justice and inequalities. More than this, I noticed that the disruption raised questions that challenged, corrected the wrongs of society or fought for change. Taking this emotion (a sense of lived experience) back to Plato and the Bhagavad Gita gave the analogies more meaning: " One can be black or white, the true aspect of the person is not the external but a deeper aspect of their self".

Another example of how our curriculum philosophy in practice comes from another of our schools is from Avanti Court Primary School. In Box 8.2, Harpreet Sahota, a highly experienced Early Years' Teacher and herself a practising Sikh, describes how this inclusive, open approach to teaching and learning fosters a knowledge-rich dialogue.

Box 8.2: Vignette by Harpreet Sahota, Assistant Headteacher at Avanti Court Primary School

The Early Years Foundation stage sets out the standards for learning, development and care for children from birth to five years of age. As part of the curriculum, Philosophy, Religious and Ethics (PRE) is embedded through a creative curriculum. Using the Avanti approach, we plan rich and exciting opportunities for children to understand the ethos and values. Each term, a value is taught and embedded where children explain the term and understand its meaning: for example, Respect:- What is respect? How can we show respect? Who would you show respect to? Why is this important? This is taught through PSHE lessons, Literacy and Understanding the World. Children are taught the teachings of Lord Chaitanya, through story-telling, roleplay, music and dance. Included in each term there is a focus of celebrating festivals, this unifies the values and character qualities. Children also have the opportunity to perform publicly with performances such as the 'Christmas Nativity'.

Living in a diverse community, children are taught all the seven major religions of the world. Children enjoy learning about the similarities and differences between the different faiths. Artefacts are explored as well as visits to the local places of worships, such as the Gurdwara, Church, Synagogue, Mosque and Temples. Respected members of the community are invited to share their knowledge of their faith to further develop children's awareness. This is through strong links with the community.

Children enjoy stories about Christmas, Diwali, Hanukkah, Easter, Vaisakhi and Eid and how people celebrate different festivals. Cooking is also embedded for e.g. children enjoy making sweet dishes such as ladoos (Indian sweets) for Diwali, chocolate nests and bread for Easter. For instance, when children make bread for Easter they spoke about how important it is for Christians to remember Jesus Christ and what he has done for the world.

In an Early Years classroom, PRE is taught in a cross curricular approach. Children are questioned to deepen their knowledge and given opportunities to write their thoughts. Children make cards using different materials for their families or friends. Teachers give children the opportunity to celebrate important festivals such as Lord Chaitanya's birthday and the Ratha Yatra festival.

Teachers continue to embed child-initiated learning within the spiritual area where children are able to write messages to Krishna or their own God (or their family members). Child-initiated learning as part of Class assemblies, including music assembly, is timetabled weekly. Prayers are read daily where children embrace their own faith or beliefs. Children are given opportunities to take part in class discussions, children are challenged if they agree or disagree their own choices, for example: Why is the big bad wolf behaving badly?

In practice: challenges and bumps on the journey

There were many false starts and changes of direction during the process and sometimes it was frustratingly slow. We realised that whilst we had a good starting point, intellectually robust and authentic, drawing from both Vedic and academic literature around dialogic teaching and learning, the articulation in classrooms required significant resources, in particular in providing effective teacher professional development. The lack of quality in established Hinduism curricula, where even key stage 4 and 5 examination board syllabi left much to be desired in terms of authenticity, meant that we had to develop a full suite of teaching plans, flipchart presentations and lesson resources. While we were aware that it was preferable for teachers to develop their own resources, we explained that they were to be considered as starting points only and not prescriptive. We decided that until we could develop teacher subject knowledge to be of a consistently high enough level, we moved to a model of subject specialist teachers for PRE.

A curriculum for hopeful futures

An inclusive approach to education, and spirituality, has always been core to the Avanti vision. It is not a naïve vision but one that builds from texts and principles that are 5000 years old and with relevance to the big questions of life and of living. These texts have synergy with the academic literature about dialogue, and therefore contemporaneous relevance. As a consequence, we have always wanted to grow beyond Hindu faith schools. Our philosophical, ethical and theological principles propel us in this direction. But it is no easy task. As we grow the family of schools within our trust, we are actively seeking to develop into a mixed-Multi Academy Trust (MAT) i.e. one that contains both denominational and non-denominational schools. What will bind these schools together is our vision for Educational excellence, Character formation and Spiritual insight.

Globalisation and societal trends are making clear the desperate need for spirituality to be made relevant and accessible in schools. Wellbeing and social cohesion are just two critical areas that will suffer if we fail to do so. We must be able to do this without defaulting to the lowest common denominator, or compromising fidelity to tradition. We know this is possible if we believe that going deeper should in fact broaden and not narrow our vision. The future of our curriculum will be critical in delivering this vision and must have relevance beyond only our Hindu schools. Value-based approaches, while remaining controversial in some academic and political circles, are now widely considered to be morally justifiable, psychologically realistic and educationally effective (Berkowitz and Bier, 2006).

We intend to also further explore secular perspectives and humanist philosophies in the curriculum overviews, which are essential to broaden our children's thinking. If we return to the story of the six blind people attempting to make sense of the obstruction in their path, all voices, all positions, all differences are needed to truly make sense of the elephant – otherwise there is an elephant in the room about which no one will speak. It is this necessary awareness of diverse diversities (Biddulph, 2017) in our thinking that the inclusivity of our curriculum design will be tested and critiqued. However, work will need to be done to broaden the exemplifications and references. With the potential to formulate a PRE curriculum drawing from global influence and with universal relevance, in many ways, this could be the most exciting part of the journey so far.

To end: Rumi asks *who looks out with my eyes?* And in so doing, identifies that we are essentially a spirit in a human body. The prison which he describes is a prison in which the material human body becomes the centre of our world. This would relate to an individualistic notion of education rather than a community of learners, with a higher moral purpose. Rumi's poetic response is to ask how the spirit might have arrived in the prison of the body and where it might end up after it leaves the prison of the body – *whoever brought me here, will have to take me home.* How we develop a curriculum in which children can make sense of themselves, who develop the values to contribute positively to the world and through relationship-making, and develop these qualities shows that the curriculum is not only what is *taught*. The curriculum is also *how we are*: it is the components of relationships, knowledge, culture, processes, skills, assessment and pedagogy. Whilst we have introduced our starting position, the reader will see that the journey is an ongoing one. For us, this is the end of the beginning.

Acknowledgments

Much of the thinking and design arose from discussions and contributions from the following people, for which we are grateful: Rasamandala Das, James Biddulph, Abala Andrews, Mark Evans, Usha Sahni OBE, Mark Bennison, Andrea Kahn, Graham Schweig, Nilamani Gor, Sunita Halai, Vandna Synghal, Srirangapriya Ramanujadasan, David Willmott, Pradip Gajjar, Lalita Jensens, Shusma Makwana, Radhika Ahuja, Sunil Randev and Harpreet Sahota.

References

Arthur, J., Kristjansson, K., Walker, D., Sanderse, W. & Jones, C. (2015) *Character Education in UK Schools*, retrieved online on 20th November 2019, http://epa pers.bham.ac.uk/1969/1/Character_Education_in_UK_Schools.pdf.

Berkowitz M. & Bier, M. (2006) What works in character education: What is known and what needs to be known. In: *Handbook of Moral and Character Education* (pp. 414–431). New York, Routledge.

Biddulph, J. (2017) The Diverse Diversities of Creative Learning at Home: Three Case Studies of Ethnic Minority Immigrant Children, Ph.D. Thesis, Cambridge, Cambridge University Library.

Bruner, J. (1996) *The Culture of Education*, Cambridge, MA, Harvard University Press.

Freire, P. (2005) *Pedagogy of the Oppressed*, New York, Continuum. Available at: https://commons.princeton.edu/inclusivepedagogy/wp-content/uploads/sit es/17/2016/07/freire_pedagogy_of_the_oppresed_ch2-3.pdf.

Gergen, K. (2009) *Relational Being: Beyond Self and Community*, New York, Oxford University Press.

Greene, M. (1998) *Releasing the Imagination: Essays on Education, the Arts and Social Change*, San Francisco, Jossey-Bass.

Lickona, T. (2015) *Forward*, retrieved online on 20th November 2019, http://epa pers.bham.ac.uk/1969/1/Character_Education_in_UK_Schools.pdf.

Phillipson, N. & Wegerif, R. (2017) *Dialogic Education: Mastering Core Concepts Through Thinking Together*, Abingdon, Routledge.

Srimad Bhagavatam (Vedic Scripture No Date). Radadesh, Belgium, Bhakti-vedanta Book Trust.

Thakura, Srila Bhaktivinode (Vedic Scripture No Date). Chapter 2. *Sri Bhajana-rahasya*, Radadesh, Belgium, Bhaktivedanta Book Trust.

Wegerif, R. (2010) *Mind Expanding*, retrieved online on 20th November 2019, http://www.rupertwegerif.name/uploads/4/3/2/7/43271253/mindexpand ing.pdf.

No mountain high enough
Using music to raise academic achievement

Phil Kirkman, Michelle Long and Luke Robbins-Ross

Introduction

This chapter discusses the role that music can play in enhancing the quality of teaching and learning in primary schools. It unlocks connections between research and practice through presenting an illustrative example of innovative practice from one school set within a broader frame of theoretical, evidence-informed knowledge which strengthens the school's curriculum design thinking. Through the story of Dixons Music Primary, an outstanding primary free academic in the northern English city of Bradford, we show how schools can raise attainment by creating a culture of music-making across the curriculum and by placing music at the heart of school life.

It is well-established that music can contribute in a significant way to children's attainment and learning in areas such as language and literacy (e.g. Yang et al., 2014), cognitive development (e.g. Schellenberg, 2014), creativity (e.g. Koutsoupidou and Hargreaves, 2009), motivation (e.g. Miksza, 2010, Hallam, 2009), physical health and wellbeing (e.g. MacDonald et al., 2012; Bailey and Davidson, 2002, 2003, 2005). It is also clear, and perhaps more significant in this context, that music makes a significant contribution to social cohesion (e.g. Hove and Risen, 2009) and through its positive impact in areas such as team work (e.g. Galarce et al., 2012), empathy (e.g. Rabinowitch et al., 2012) and self-efficacy (e.g. Israel, 2012). At the same time, however, although music education is still a statutory entitlement in the UK, many students, parents and teachers raise concerns that is being increasingly 'squeezed out' of many school curricular, citing issues such as finding cuts, damaging accountability systems and its status being affected by unpopular and curriculum reforms (APPGME, 2019).

Alongside each other, these ideas reveal a striking contradiction. That music can contribute in so many significant ways to a happy, holistic and healthy education whilst being effectively cut out of many children's education is both bemusing and perhaps inevitable. Schools exist in political cultures and constantly face competing priorities. On the one hand, teachers and school leaders know their children, their parents and their communities. They share their successes and their failures. They know their needs and their strengths. In this way, schools are well-placed to help individuals and communities to grow and develop. At the same time, school leaders know that their success is measured crudely in terms of the academic attainment of their students. At best this is limiting; at worst everything becomes a luxury apart from language, maths and science. One may argue that this stems from the wider issue of international comparisons which take the same crude approach to evaluation (OECD, 2019) but this is beyond the scope of this chapter. What this does mean, however, is that in the absence of national leadership that effectively safeguards a broad and balanced education for all, it falls to school leaders and teachers to take up this challenge. The responsibility and the decision that all school leaders must make is between the need to promote a holistic education and risk falling foul of accountability systems that fail to account for such 'luxuries', or the pressure to play it safe, 'tick the boxes' and provide access to learning that neglects, amongst other things, the power of music to transform lives and to build communities. In this context, the story of Dixons Music Primary is not only heartening but is noteworthy because it reveals that it is not only possible but that it can be academically advantageous for schools to place music at the heart of a school.

Building the case for music and how it can remove barriers

"Ain't No Mountain High Enough" is an R&B/soul song written by Nickolas Ashford and Valerie Simpson in 1966. The original 1967 version was a top 20 hit in the UK and the metaphors within the song are used to inspire not only a sense of community endeavour but also a vision for children that is aspirational and a passionate commitment that nothing can and should stop children from achieving in education. The academy carefully selects its range of songs to ensure there is a metaphorical link to aspiration and climbing the mountain to university. But, of course, the school's vision and purpose is not based simply on the lyrics from a popular song. In this chapter, the authors, two of whom are senior leaders in the academy, introduce the children and the community they serve through vignettes which bring to life how they work. Together with an academic with music expertise, we problematise the challenges of serving a diverse multi-ethnic, though predominantly Muslim community, and consider the way that music serves as a vehicle that helps both to define and to articulate how and why they work as they do.

> Context for the Dixons Music Primary:
>
> - All our academies serve areas of Bradford and Leeds in areas of high social disadvantage.
> - At the Music Primary, 50% of our students come from the five poorest wards in Bradford, which are also some of the most impoverished areas in the country.
> - The large majority of our students are Pakistani heritage students, and this group of students are often seen to perform poorly in national data sets.
> - Whilst we recognise our context and value the diversity of our students, we do not use the challenges faced as excuses for low expectation or aspiration.
> - We have taken our ideas from the best schools across the country and globe as well as look outward to successful businesses to see how they grow and innovate.

We noted above that music in education matters (Alexander, 2010; Hallam, 2015). This data extract illustrates how much it can matter to families and to children. Music matters because children find immense pleasure in musical participation and moreover it is a way of building a sense of self, community and cultural identity. It is a vital part of childhood (Burnard, 2017). Children make up music in the playground, at home, in the classroom; they are engaged in a natural 'musicking' by playing musical toys, tapping out rhythms, singing along with others on the school bus, listening to music at home alone and together; it is part of cultural and religious events (Small, 1998). Some of this benefit is articulated by the parent of Ayesha.

Child 'Ayesha' – Year 5 (aged, 10)

My daughter has grown a lot in her confidence since doing music. When I saw her in class she was asked to read in front of the class and this is something she would never have done before learning the drums and singing with DMP Young Voices. She loves being a part of DMP Young Voices and singing in competitions has been a rewarding experience. But it is her confidence mainly. She has to be disciplined and focused but through something she loves and now a genuine love of music is there that I would never have been able to…. I could not afford to pay for lessons but to see her as a musician and perform to an audience makes me so proud. Staff give 110% and make sure she succeeds.

At Music Primary, we recognised that music could become the powerful vehicle for driving up standards and personal development forward. We knew also that a whole school approach to music would need 'buy in' from the whole team and school community. We first attended to this by designing the ethos and culture, constructing 'spaces' that would symbolise the value we would give to music, to instrumental learning and to the effort required to improve in learning an instrument. There is a growing body of evidence that indicates music can exert a positive impact on cognitive development and learning:

> Many studies have shown how learning music uses similar processes as learning sounds and patterns, which in turn can aid in the development of language and reading. Crucially, further studies have shown that if structured and long-term music making is provided at an early stage (i.e. pre-school) then these benefits are even greater.
>
> *(Hallam, 2015: p. 2)*

There is also evidence which suggests that learning an instrument can impact positively on academic outcomes. For all children everywhere, and the economically deprived community we serve, our curriculum design decisions were influenced by an unwavering belief that every child, no matter who they were, where they came from, their background or family economic position, should be given every chance to pursue education at University level or apprenticeship route. We were empowered by the evidence that:

> Better academic attainment is often achieved by those learning to play a musical instrument; however, a key reason for this may be greater motivation more generally. Motivation is linked to self-perceptions of ability and self-efficacy (i.e. how able a person feels to carry out tasks), therefore, the higher a person's motivation, the bigger the gains in achievement. Musical practice is well placed to increase and nurture motivation in children and young people (Hallam, 2015), but again there is evidence that children must enjoy their music making in order to sustain motivation.
>
> *(Hallam, 2009: p. 2)*

In his 2011 review of music education in England for the DfE, Darren Henley stated that he was "convinced of the positive effect that music, both as an academic subject, taught in the classroom, and as a participative activity, in and out of the classroom can have on young people's lives" (Henley, 2011: p. 4). Other research supports Henley's conclusion: for example, in their review of literature from 2010–2013 (NFER, 2000), the Art Council found that:

- Taking part in structured music activities improves attainment in maths, early language acquisition and early literacy.
- Students from low-income families who take part in arts activities at school are three times more likely to get a degree than children who do not engage in arts activities in school.
- Employability of students who study arts subjects is higher and they are more likely to stay in employment.

Another earlier study by Harvard Project Zero in 2001 also found some links to the studying of music and improved academic attainment; they found that listening to music gave rise to a temporary improvement in spatial–temporal reasoning. More interestingly, they found stronger links between learning to play an instrument and the effect on spatial reasoning. The review suggested more research was needed to satisfy claims that learning to play an instrument had a positive impact on attainment in reading and maths.

In recent times, music education often hits the headlines for the wrong reasons, with the uptake of General Certificate of Secondary Education (GCSE) music on a steady decline and funding cuts to services resulting in so-called postcode lotteries leading to many children receiving a poor-quality music education. However, there are a plethora of research studies promoting the positive effects that a high-quality music and arts education can have on not only academic achievement but on mental wellbeing, positive school culture, improved community cohesion and the British economy. Indeed, the Cambridge Primary Review (Alexander, 2010), which drew on extensive review of national and international research evidence, concluded in its recommendations for policy and practice that the arts and music education must be central to the experience of primary- aged children and that it should happen in schools.

Government policy

It is encouraging that in recent years, the government has declared that music does matter. Although one could argue that this assertion would not be necessary if warnings about the damaging effects of successive curriculum reforms had been heeded (APPGME, 2019). Music is still a subject that must be studied as part of the National Curriculum in Key Stages 1 to 3 and whilst academies and free schools are not required to follow the National Curriculum, the government *has* stated that music should form part of a 'broad and balanced' curriculum. In 2011, the Henley review of music education in England acknowledged that, along with the primary benefits of music (improved subject knowledge and skill in the subject), so called 'secondary benefits' of learning music were also apparent. These secondary benefits included increased self-esteem, improved behaviour and social skills as well as improved attainment in numeracy, literacy and language. Following on from the findings of the Henley Review, the National Plan for Music Education was published later that year. The review highlights that most children will have their first experience of music at school. Several studies have shown that whilst music touches the lives of all young people, disadvantaged students are particularly likely to benefit (e.g. Devroop, 2012).

At the same time, however, disadvantaged students also do not have the resources necessary to ensure continued access to music (APPGME, 2019). Furthermore, the creation of the EBacc ostensibly to ensure access to 'core subjects' in practice had the effect of limiting access to a broad and balanced curriculum (Gill and Williamson, 2016). Thus, while it is 'important'; music is clearly not considered important enough to safeguard for all students at a national level. Yet, in contrast to this, Dixons Music Primary's most recent Key Stage 2 results disadvantaged students' attainment was higher than other students nationally. Thus, as well as safeguarding breadth and balance, it seems our musical ethos also promotes success in so called 'core subjects'. Although it is not certain to what extent this trend is *determined* by our music-infused curriculum, it is evident that the curriculum promotes wider achievement. Hearteningly, her Majesty's Inspectorate for Schools (Ofsted) have now recognised that students' involvement in music engages and re-engages pupils, increasing their self-esteem and maximises their progress in education and not just in music (Ofsted Inspection Framework, 2019).

In the next section, the senior leaders who co-wrote the chapter describe how music is employed across the school and how they created a place in which music making had a significant role to play in raising aspirations for the whole school community.

Mountaineering: The Dixons Music Primary – a place for music making

Dixons Music Primary is part of the Dixons Academies Trust whose collective mission is to challenge educational and social disadvantage in the North. The high performing Multi Academy Trust does this by establishing high-performing non-faith academies that maximise attainment, value diversity, develop character and build a sense of cultural capital. It is a 'high mountain' we have committed to climb! Since we opened, our school has become a popular, inner-city primary school in Bradford, serving students from some of the poorest wards in the country. The academy opened as a free school in 2012 with just 30 reception students and is now oversubscribed with students from Early Years to Year 6. The academy is values-driven, underpinned by strict routines and rigour. The academy mission is simple: "The academy ensured that all students succeeded at university, thrived in a top job and had a great life". It is purposefully written in the past tense, as it is how the academy wishes to be remembered.

One of the most fundamental elements of Dixons Music Primary's success is that it is a school built on its three values of:

- Hard work (we do whatever it takes for as long as it takes).
- Independence (we are resilient learners and are always willing to have a go).
- Enjoyment (we enjoy our learning and behave well so that others can enjoy theirs).

We saw that these guiding principles could be aligned, and indeed supported, by learning an instrument and being involved in music: the determination, independent practise on an instrument and resulting enjoying learning are present in music making. Our staff and students alike know these values and their definitions. The senior team recruit people who are aligned to these values and the academy's mission. Staff do not need to be musical themselves, but they need to show an appreciation for the subject and understand the role music plays within the academy.

The first idea of a music specialist free school for the Dixons Academies Trust came from the CEO's visit to some of New York's most influential charter schools in the early 2000s. The charter schools are similar to the English 'free school' movement and are set up to serve students in disadvantaged areas and are free from local authority control. In particular, the KIPP (Knowledge is Power Program) schools were found to be unique in that in some of the schools, all students learned an instrument and formed an orchestra. All students visit a university each year throughout their time in Key Stage 1 and Key Stage 2. It is important for all students to experience what university 'feels' like and gives them a memorable learning experience which they will take with them throughout their schooling.

In 2000, the NfER study found that the arts were "seen by many members of senior management in schools to impact on the whole school ethos, mainly by encouraging a positive cohesive atmosphere through enhancing pupils' enjoyment, self-esteem and achievement" (NfER, 2000). These findings were supported by the UNESCO research in 2003, who found that the arts helped to develop a large range of life skills and interpersonal skills including improving tolerance, acceptance and appreciation of others (NfER, 2000).

As a music specialist academy, the senior team felt it was important to make it clear why the specialism of music had been chosen. They also found that common perceptions from visitors were that music would be a central part of every session throughout the day, which it is not. Rather, music is a targeted feature of the educational experience of every child. Building from the research base (Hallam, 2009), our music vision evolved to become the following:

> Music Primary *uses music* to raise standards of achievement in reading, writing and mathematics. It is also at the heart of our joyful and disciplined school culture. Singing is used to develop oracy. Performance is used to develop confidence and character. Learning to read music helps accelerate literacy and numeracy. Ensemble is used to promote interaction and co-operation. Instrumental work develops co-ordination and fine motor skills.

It is also important to recognise that there is a relationship between culture, society and forms of power (Bourdieu, 1990), that people in responsibility have the power to make decisions on the communities or society in their midst. And that these decisions can be unbalanced in terms of power and ownership. For example, in deciding to have music as central to our curriculum and ethos, we could potentially be advocating for a white middle-class set of cultural values that were at odds with the diverse communities we serve. However, like Wright and Davies (2010), we attempted to design the curriculum aware and critiquing of our own social practices – "human beings constantly seeking to preserve or enhance their own interest" (p. 43); secondly, to understand different forms of cultural capital and that music was a form of cultural capital, and thirdly, that culture always has the potential to be 'othered' and different cultures to be differentiated – as high or low, us and them, for example. Do state-funded schools represent the high culture and our community the low? We did expect great things from our students and saw music as a vehicle through which to challenge more children to aspire – to metaphorically climb that learning mountain. We did want to find pathways for our children to be able to gain access to higher education and lead positive successful lives. In this way, we saw that, "the social world [is] constructed from past practices and provided a space for the creation of present and future ones" (Wright and Davies, 2010: p. 43). Our curriculum needed to help create new futures for our children and their community. One of our parent's view of the inclusion and celebration of diversity that our music curriculum design brought to their child suggests a cultural awareness in our approach:

Talking about Mohammed – Year 6, aged 11

He has become a brilliant musician through the support of the staff and the opportunities they give him he has improved his self-confidence and made him focus his energy into mastering the drums. He loves the small group lessons and has built positive relationships and has now less corrections since starting drums. His behavior at home also improved. He has been able to sit for externally accredited exams and gain merits on his certificates – something I probably wouldn't have expected when he first said he wanted to learn the drums. He appreciates **different styles of music** and compares different songs, talking enthusiastically at home about the similarities and **differences about people also**. Staff are role models and my son particularly likes listening to the staff choir in assemblies.

Mohammed's parent seems to value the musical learning happening in school because it was impacting positively on his attitude and wider awareness of diversity. There was almost a self-perpetuating cycle of musical success, improved social and emotional outcomes that led to better self-discipline and attitudes to learning.

Climbing the mountain: the practical steps we took to teach/reach the summit in curriculum design

At Dixons Music Primary, we have tried to take the best ideas from academies, schools, the independent sector and abroad. Music helps our pupils to develop self-discipline and a growth mindset – to climb the mountain to university, succeed when they get there, thrive in a top job and have a great life. A step up that mountain every day; a little bit of progress every day. We use music to raise standards of achievement in reading, writing and mathematics. It is also at the heart of the academy's joyful and disciplined school culture.

Having established our values and guiding vision for the school, we looked to the principles upon which our curriculum would be designed. We wanted every opportunity for our children to access powerful knowledge which would open doors and maximise their life chances. We arrived at the following:

- We challenge social inequality by instilling shared and powerful knowledge.
- Children need powerful knowledge to understand and interpret the world, and to think in new and unexpected ways. Without it, they remain dependent upon those who have it.
- Shared and powerful knowledge is verified through learned communities e.g. universities, research and subject associations.
- Powerful academic knowledge is cognitively superior to everyday knowledge, transcending and liberating students from their daily experience.
- Shared knowledge is a foundation for a just and sustainable democracy. Citizens educated together share an understanding of our common values, and can understand, cooperate and shape the world together.[1]

We brought together the key aspects of the curriculum design that needed to be addressed and worked on so that we could demonstrate clear progressions. Figure 9.1 shows these aspects:

	Curriculum	Vocal	Percussion	Woodwind
Content	Declarative knowledge (facts; knowing that something is the case; what we think about)			
Performing	Non-declarative or procedural knowledge (skills and processes; knowing how to do something; what we think with			
Creating				
Understanding	Declarative knowledge			
All underpinned in the beginning by an adaptation of the ISM's Progression Framework				

We started by stating clearly our purpose and what we wanted for our students. The musical grammar of each subject is given high status; the specifics of what we want students to learn matter and the traditions of subject disciplines are respected. To this, we drew from Hirsch's knowledge curriculum as a basis upon which we would develop our music curriculum. We embraced the position that:

- Skills and understanding are seen as forms of knowledge and we do not believe that there are any real generic skills that can be taught outside of specific knowledge domains.

Progression Framework

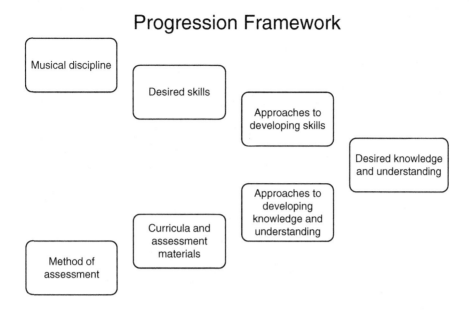

Figure 9.1 Music Progression Framework

- The curriculum should be planned vertically and horizontally giving thought to the optimum knowledge sequence for building secure schema.
- The curriculum should be designed to be remembered in detail: to be stored in our students' long-term memories so that they can later build on it forming ever wider and deeper schema. As a result, a good knowledge-rich curriculum embraces learning from cognitive science about memory, forgetting and the power of retrieval practice.
- The curriculum is owned by students from all faiths and backgrounds, not by any one. The selected content should conform to shared cultural agreements of what is considered valuable to know. It is the entitlement of all and we resist parental opt-outs.
- The curriculum should embrace and value the most powerful knowledge from a variety of cultures and traditions.
- At each phase, the curriculum should focus on closing gaps, early intervention and developing the core literacy and numeracy skills for success at that level.
- Both in and out of the classroom, the curriculum should build the hard work, diligence and resilience necessary for success in life.
- The curriculum should introduce students to new experiences and powerful knowledge beyond the classroom and outside the academy to broaden their horizons and to prepare them fully for later life.
- Curriculum breadth and academic rigour are key to our mission: "Imparting broad knowledge to all children is the single most effective way to narrow the gap between demographic groups through schooling" (Hirsch, 2006: p. 5).

We then explored the **nature of musical discipline** asking the question, "what is needed to be a successful musician?" For example, preparing children to practice regularly needed to be encouraged and expected from the outset. We then narrowed the discussion to consider the **desired skills**, the different **pedagogical approaches** we would need to take to develop these skills and which would lead to the **intended knowledge and understanding** of and about music. Alongside these aspects, we considered **methods of assessment**, **curriculum materials** which could help develop skills and knowledge, and in the same way as pedagogic approaches to teaching the skills of musicianship, to identify approaches for the development of **knowledge and understanding**. This is an ongoing piece of work and as an iterative process requires ongoing discussion. Having explored these aspects, we articulated our curriculum design intention devised by the academy's Head of Music, Clair Ward.

Intention of the music curriculum: a powerful, knowledge-rich practical curriculum

- By the end of their all-through education, a student of Music at Dixons Trinity Academy, our sister academy, will:
    - Know how to read and interpret traditional and modern notation.
    - Be able to apply practical instrumental techniques on the Keyboard, Drum Kit, Woodwind, Ukulele/Guitar and the Voice, as a soloist and as part of an ensemble.
    - Understand the social and cultural importance of music and its impact across different genres and centuries.
- Our uniting 'sentence' is "The Music department ensured that every student has a sound understanding of musical concepts, an experience of mastering at least one instrument, and the confidence to apply these theories to any given musical situation".
    - In order to achieve a true understanding of Music topics have been intelligently sequenced based on the following rationale:
    - A sound vocal tradition is established in Reception and developed throughout KS1 and KS2.
    - Rhythmic work is introduced in KS1 on individual drums, and this leads to Drum Kit skills in KS2. Tuned percussion is added through the medium of Charanga, and these skills are transferred to Keyboard in upper KS2 through a bespoke written curriculum.
    - Woodwind is introduced in KS2, starting with Ocarina, and progressing to Fife (via Penny Whistle and Recorder); until Flute, Clarinet and Saxophone can be introduced in upper KS2.

- These instrumental studies are interleaved with curriculum lessons, covering historical styles, cultural differences and creative concepts (such as composing and appraising); maximising students' emersion in Music.
- KS3 Music lessons are sequenced to allow students to learn about the musical elements through a variety of genres of music. Listening, Performing, Composing and Appraising are covered in each unit.
- KS4 is divided into a pre-course skills year (9), and then the 4-unit BTEC course (10 & 11).
- In terms of instrumental music, students are taught basic skills, notations and techniques. As they become more proficient, they are moved into groups to allow for peer mentoring and coaching.

- The Music curriculum will address social disadvantage by addressing gaps in pupils' knowledge and skills by:
  - Ensuring they have the powerful knowledge and skills to become confident musicians with the courage to explore musical styles and instruments.
  - Promoting underrepresented cultures and styles, such as world music and orchestral classics.
  - Ensuring that all students, regardless of any additional needs, can understand and access key skills and concepts through practical and visual clarity of instruction and practice.
  - Community context.

- At KS2, KS3 and KS4, our belief is that homework should be an interleaved revision of powerful knowledge that has been modelled and taught in lessons. This knowledge is recalled and applied through a range of low-stakes quizzing and practice.

- A true love of Music involves learning about the domain of Music. We teach beyond the specification requirements, but do ensure students are well prepared to be successful in GCSE examinations:
  - We teach a range of genres and styles, from Bach to Beatles, including music from different countries and cultures, over a variety of instruments.
  - Independent listening enquiry is encouraged by the department 'listening station', where students can hear different and related pieces outside of their official learning time.
  - Full through vocal curriculum with Vocal specialists from Reception to Year 11.
  - 100% students learn to play three musical instruments (Drums, Woodwind, Keyboard) during KS1 and KS2.
  - 35% of students play a musical instrument.

- Co-curricular is offered to KS3 and KS4. Students are encouraged to explore new and different instruments and to take control of the rehearsal process.
- Dixons Music Primary (DMP) musicians have gained Rock School practical qualifications, including two students gaining UCAS points for passing post grade 6 examinations. Thirty DMP students passed with Merit and Distinction Vocal and Drum Kit exams, including three at Grade 3.
- A culture of autonomous independent practice is developing in the Music department. Year 5 students regularly come through to DTA to practice along with a backing track in the practice rooms to prepare for their next practical lesson, developing time keeping skills and independence.
- A wide variety of extra-curricular groups are available for students to join, including: Soul Band, Choir, Chamber Choir, Rock Band, Samba, Music Theory classes and Senior/Junior Young Voices.
- The Music department hosts three showcases each academic year. These are co-run by BTEC students and include performances from DMP and DTA musicians. The standard of performance is increasing with each showcase.
- Students are invited annually to perform at Multi Academy Trust (MAT) collaboration concerts, including the upcoming Dixons Conference.
- The instrumental team are based across the MAT. This allows for Quality Assurance and continuity between primary and secondary phases.
- The department hosts an annual London Theatre residential, allowing our musicians to experience the west end, professional performances and London theatre workshops.
- Skill trackers are used to track progress in curriculum and instrumental lessons. Accurate monitoring allows for 'live' intervention to be put in place during a practical session. Students are responsible for their mastery time and have autonomy over their practical assessments.
- Online learning platforms are used for students to support their progress in and out of the classroom.

Further information

- All through curriculum overview.
- Long term plans.
- 100% sheets.
- Schemes of Work.

Organising the curriculum: Practical steps

Reflections from a teacher

The music room is where our most vulnerable students gravitate. Why? It's their social, emotional and mental safe haven. Music's nurturing quality has a profound impact on allowing them to connect with peers in a unique way. It equips students to have the highest of standards; never wanting to make a mistake in a solo performance or performing at 95% competitions with DMP Young Voices (academy choir) just isn't enough. Music demands the strive for perfection – our music mantra – don't practice until you get it right, practice until you can't get it wrong.

Having brought together our thinking through progression and intention documents, we looked to how we would practically implement the curriculum and how we would deploy and organise staff. We wanted to foster collaboration with music services delivered by high-quality subject specialists, working in cross-cutting teams to create the richest narrative possible for their students.

We operate differently from a traditional primary school. The students have a longer school day, beginning school at 8.00am and finishing at 3.45pm. This allows students to receive musical tuition as part of the school day. The senior team are often asked how the school affords its music tuition and the answer is through strategic deployment of staff. For example, there are no teaching assistants in Key Stage 2; the senior team teach several year groups in a 'lecture' style to enable teachers to have feedback or specialist intervention time.

Singing features as an important part of the school day. We strongly believe that singing positively impacts on oracy skills. We use performance to develop confidence and character because, "at the heart of collective and connected learning experiences, particularly in the performing arts, lies the role and nature of participation" (Burnard: p. 60). Learning to read music seemed also to help accelerate literacy and numeracy (though we have not researched this robustly). We noted that through performance, children and their teachers could be "empowered participants as performers, arrangers, improvisers" (p. 61) and that, "even performing small and personal performances provides an interactive and participatory means for children to claim ownership of learning and knowledge creation through active involvement in its presentation, whereby they are enabled by everyone to share and collaborate" (p. 61). We noted that ensemble work definitely promoted interaction and co-operation and this was balanced with instrumental work which developed co-ordination and fine motor skills.

Using specialists

Because most primary teachers in the UK are generalists, we believed that it would be difficult for them to teach music to a higher enough level to provide the rich experiences that we expected for our children. Indeed, research suggests that staff need to be highly qualified and trained in the subject of music. Our students receive between three to four music and performance lessons a week. These are all delivered by music and performing arts specialists. Our PE and Performing Arts specialist teacher is funded partly through the Sports Premium grant and produces fantastic showcases each term. Every week, each pupil receives instrumental, vocal and ensemble tuition in a mixture of small and large group tuition which is delivered by specialist music teachers. During their music lessons, children learn technical, musical and performance skills. All pupils have Performing Arts lessons each week where they work together to showcase their skills in performances throughout the year. This may be similar to other schools, but by considering music as a vital tool through which to develop academic, social and personal skills meant that we would not tolerate second best experiences for our children.

Being co-located with Dixons Trinity Academy, the first secondary free school to receive an Outstanding judgement by Ofsted has many benefits. Being able to partner with our secondary school was a significant leaver to develop our musicianship work in the primary school. The Head of Music at Dixons Trinity now oversees the music provision and music team at Dixons Music Primary. This all-through approach to music has taken shape organically and the anticipation is for our cohort to be able to sit GCSE music in year 9. Being co-located is also particularly beneficial to the specialist staff for their own professional development as they have the opportunity to teach at Key Stage 3 whilst secondary staff teach from Reception to Year 6. The music team consists of the Head of Music at Dixons Trinity Academy, a specialist singing and music teacher (full time); a percussion teacher (part time) and a specialist music curriculum teacher (full time).

We engage with the Bradford Music Education Hub and have been accredited by the Hub as a Music Mark School for showing a commitment to developing the best possible environment for a child's music education. We were commended for showing:

- Evidence of a willingness to engage in development conversations related to improving music provision.
- Recognition of the value of music education as part of a broad and balanced curriculum.
- A strategy for music in place which provides for all children.[2]

Our mantra for students 'Don't practice until you get it right, practice until you can't get it wrong' is used to intrinsically motivate students.

We are also fortunate to have an extremely committed staff team and all staff rehearse once a fortnight as part of the staff choir, DMP Voices. The rehearsals are an opportunity to come together as a team and rehearse for a performance for students each half term. It also allows skills such as conducting to be taught for the professional development of staff.

The academy has a fantastically inclusive school choir, DMP Young Voices, who recently performed at the Manchester MEN Arena. We were selected as one of four schools to perform at the BBC Music Day in June 2017. We were recently shortlisted for Pulse Radio's Christmas Choir 2018 and 2019 having won the competition last year and performed at the Broadway Centre, Bradford in November. Some students who have more challenging behaviours are members of the choir and have flourished in terms of their ability to persevere, work as part of a team and demonstrate a genuine enthusiasm and ability in terms of their singing. We use ABRSM Music Medals and Rock School examinations to ensure students are gaining something meaningful from their hard work and commitment.

Singing assemblies take place weekly and learn a variety of songs all linked to our values and mission of climbing the mountain to university. As a Makaton Friendly accredited school, we place great emphasis on learning Makaton in our singing assemblies to allow students to communicate in an alternative way.

Training non-specialists

The Charanga Musical School Scheme, which is used in Years R-4, provides teachers with week-by-week lessons for each year group in the school from ages 5–11. It is ideal for specialist and non-specialist teachers and provides lesson plans, assessment, clear progression, and engaging and exciting whiteboard resources for every lesson. The Scheme supports all the requirements of the national curriculum and is in line with published Ofsted guidance. We use ABRSM Music Medals and Rock School examinations to ensure students are gaining something meaningful from their hard work and commitment. We have a 100% pass rate for all students entered into external music examinations in 2018/19, which is something the academy is very proud of.

Collaboration

The Trust have invested in the value of the creative arts through the appointment of a Director of Music who works closely with all schools across the Trust to maximise the expertise that each academy has to offer whether it be staffing or curriculum development. This was particularly successful when the primary schools in the MAT as well as schools from outside the MAT worked collaboratively on a vocal project culminating in a performance at Dixons City Academy. Students also perform at Dixons Trinity Showcases each term, which is an opportunity for them to see first-hand what a secondary will feel like.

Mountain rescue: inclusion for all

Inclusion is key for the success of our students. There is strong evidence that music plays a key role in children's lives (Sloboda et al., 2009). We see first-hand how music generates feelings of wellbeing and helps children work through different emotions. In our experience, music is used for regulating emotion and can help induce positive mental states and achieve positive moods. We have seen the positive impact music has on helping students cope with negative moods and emotions. We ensure students are exposed to a variety of genres of music on a daily basis; the most common activity to regulate mood is listening to music. Research suggests that adults who play an instrument say that the best way to regulate mood is through listening to music (Saarikallio, 2006).

The academy has developed sensory provision for students with sensory needs and music is a key vehicle of success. A student's understanding of music both in written and auditory can aid in the way we communicate. For students with Autistic Spectrum Disorder, this could mean learning a new lyric from a song, or a clearer understanding as to how to express themselves in a social situation based on the meaning of the lyrics. We have based our curriculum, as we do with our routines and rituals, around the most vulnerable students. We ensure that we empower students with ASD can face barriers particularly within social settings. Small groups allow students to listen to music together and develop their confidence and are comfortable to comment or sing with peers. Performing arts lessons at the academy also help to stimulate a student's sensory system and allow them to develop fine motor skills. Music is a unique form of communication that can change the way pupils feel, think and act and has had a positive effect on students with selective mutism allowing them to express themselves in a supportive and collaborative way.

Outcomes

The academy saw its first set of Key Stage 2 results in July 2019, which placed its students above national figures for attainment in reading, writing, maths and Grammar Punctuation and Spelling. The combined measure of students achieving the expected standard in Reading Writing Maths was 15% above national figures, with 80% achieving this. Music has played a key part of instilling a joyful and disciplined school culture, which has been carefully crafted and impacted positively on student outcomes at all key stages.

Inclusion and wellbeing

The positive outcomes of actively engaging with music in terms of wellbeing is well documented. The academy actively promotes the benefits of music on physical health and wellbeing. For our more vulnerable students, carefully planned musical activities (including extra-curricular clubs) leads to a sense of accomplishment, greater determination and perseverance. A 7-year-old student was able to better cope with their anger and express their emotions more effectively through a bespoke 1:1 music intervention. The academy has seen huge benefits in terms of discipline, relaxation, overcoming difficulties, communication as well as the ability to work with others. Several of the academy's students have benefited from taking part in small group singing to overcome a trauma they had faced. It allowed them to re-build their self-esteem, trust and a sense of identity.

Reading: music as a vehicle for learning sounds and reading

We started to see that music was contributing to improvements in phonological awareness. Phonological awareness, including segmenting and blending sounds, are similar to the skills required to understand and distinguish between rhythm, harmony and melody. We looked at a number of studies exploring the effect music has on phonological ability. Strait and Kraus (2014) talk about how school aged students and adults who have a strong musical awareness are able to make stronger distinctions between syllables compared to non-music students. The academy's programme of study for instrumental tuition is supported by research by Chobert et al. (2011) which shows students who have music lessons for at least four years are more accurate in discriminating syllables which vary in duration and frequency compared to students who have not had lessons. An adept knowledge of music increases the ability to interpret speech rhythms and 8-year-olds with musical training outperformed those without .

Weak musical performance has also been associated with a delay in the processing of speech sounds. A study by Gromko (2005) attempted to demonstrate causality i.e. that by actively making music, speech perception is enhanced. He studied primary school children who received four months of music instruction for 30 minutes (once per week). This included active music making with movement to emphasise the steady beat, rhythm and pitch. Students who received the tuition also showed significantly greater gains in phonemic awareness when compared to the control group.

Some studies have reported the importance of both rhythmic and pitch perception in the development of reading skills. Anvari and colleagues (2002) studied 50 four- and 50 five-year-olds and found that both rhythm and pitch perception skills predicted early reading performance in four-year-olds even after taking account of variance due to phonological awareness. In five-year-olds, only pitch perception predicted early reading performance after accounting for phonological awareness.

In Key Stage 1, where musical activities involve learning to read notation, it can be argued that there is a direct link to reading text. Singing as it involves reading predicable text, segmenting words into syllables so that lyrics can be matched to music or recognising patterns has been proposed as one possible explanation for the improvement of literacy following musical activity.

Listening

The academy has spent time researching the impact music has on a child's listening ability. Using music as the learning media has allowed students to embed knowledge through chants and rhymes. The academy's values are sung for students to listen to in weekly assemblies. Students' appreciation of each other's performances has improved greatly due to their ability to appraise through careful listening of performances. From reception, students are taught to listen and respond to performances both in full class and small groups. This allows them to be attentive listeners and begins the process for becoming adept appraisers.

Communicating

Music is one of the few ways in which students can connect with each other without language; it is a way in which cultures cannot only identify themselves but also communicate with each other and find common ground. Think of a culture that's very different to your own; one that you have noticed for some reason or other, but don't know very much about. You'll probably get an instant mental picture of the people of that culture and perhaps have some impression of their language, art and music, too. These sights and sounds can leave a deep impression on us. The sights and sounds of a particular culture may affect us without our fully understanding the meaning of their importance within that culture.

Final thoughts: more climbing

By embracing music as a key feature in their educational offer, Dixons have expressed a confidence and an intention that children's sense of identity (what Plato might have called their soul) and their ability to imagine new possibilities for themselves and their communities (the flight of the imagination as Plato tells us) would come to fruition. The expression of belief in this collaborative endeavor is communicated and understood in and through music and the related activities – what Small (2011) calls Musiking – not just to students but also to parents and their community. In this way, they not only reinforce children's aspirations but also bolster the belief of the community in the systems and structures that can support or that can prevent access to opportunities for development. In short, through music they bring hope. Dixons have grappled with the logistics, the practicalities and the risks of investing in a subject that is undervalued or seen as an unnecessary luxury; that is frequently not given sufficient time in Initial Teacher Education; that is widely under-resourced. They also know that there is more to be done to include even more diverse music from a variety of cultural traditions and to support the professional learning and development of largely generalist teachers. Yet, what they have seen at Dixons Music Primary is validation of the messages, from what are now decades of research, about the significance of and urgent need for properly embedding music within and across the primary curriculum; not as an 'add-on' but as a central and vital hallmark of any high-quality education. So, whether at Dixons Music Primary or across the wider Primary sector, it is clear that there are still more mountains to climb, more valleys to traverse and more rivers to cross before we get to a place where we have realised the full potential of music in and across the primary curriculum.

Notes

1 These bullet points are adapted from work by Carolyn Roberts, Headteacher, Thomas Tallis School
2 Adapted from 2018 blogs by Tom Sherrington https://teacherhead.com/

References

Alexander, R. (2010). *Children, their World, their Education: Final Report and Recommendations of the Cambridge Primary Review*. Oxon: Routledge.

Anvari, S. & Trainor, L. & Woodside, J. & Levy, B. (2002). Relations among musical skills, phonological processing, and early reading ability in preschool children. *Journal of Experimental Child Psychology*, 83, 111–130.

APPGME (2019). *Music Education: State of the Nation. Report by the All-Party Parliamentary Group for Music Education, the Incorporated Society of Musicians and the University of Sussex*. London: ISM.

Bailey, B.A. & Davidson, J.W. (2002). Adaptive characteristics of group singing: Perceptions form members of a choir for homeless men, *Musicae Scientiae*, 6(2), 221–256.

Bailey, B.A. & Davidson, J.W. (2003). Amateur group singing as a therapeutic agent, *Nordic Journal of Music Therapy*, 12(1), 18–32.

Bailey, B.A. & Davidson, J.W. (2005). Effects of group singing and performance for marginalised and middle-class singers, *Psychology of Music*, 33(3), 269–303.

Bourdieu, P. & Passeron, J-C. (1990). *Reproduction in Education, Society and Culture*. London: Sage.

Burnard, P. (2017). Teaching music creatively. In P. Burnard (ed.) *Teaching Music Creatively*. Taylor & Francis.

Chobert, J., Marie, C., François, C., Schön, D. & Besson, M. (2011). Enhanced passive and active processing of syllables in musician children. *Journal of Cognitive Neuroscience*, 23(12), 3874–3887. https://doi.org/10.1162/jocn_a_00088.

Devroop, K. (2012). The social-emotional impact of instrumental music performance on economically disadvantaged South African students, *Music Education Research*, 14(4), 407–416.

Galarce, E., Berardi, L. & Sanchez, B. (2012). *OASIS, OAS Orchestra Programme for Youth at Risk in the Caribbean - Music for Social Change: Final Report*: Washington, DC: Organization of American States.

Gill, T. & Williamson, J. (2016). *Uptake of GCSE Subjects 2015*. Statistics report series no. 107, Cambridge Assessment. http://www.cambridgeassessment.org.uk/Images/307016-uptake-of-gcse-subjects-2015.pdf. (accessed 1st April 2020)

Gromko, J.E. (2005). The effect of music instruction on phonemic awareness in beginning readers. *Journal for Research in Music Education*, 53(3), 199–209.

Hallam, S. (2009). Motivation to learn. In: S. Hallam, I. Cross & M. Thaut (eds) *Handbook of Psychology of Music* (pp. 285–294). Oxford: Oxford University Press.

Henley, D. (2011). *Music Education in England for the Department for Education and the Department for Culture, Media and Sport*. London: Her Majesty's Print

Hallam (2015). The power of music: a research synthesis of the impact of actively making music on the intellectual, social and personal development of children and young people. https://www.researchgate.net/publication/273126443_The_power_of_music_a_research_synthesis_of_the_impact_of_actively_mak ing_music_on_the_intellectual_social_and_personal_development_of_child ren_and_young_people (accessed 1st April 2020).

Hirsch, E.D. (2006). *The Knowledge Deficit: Closing the Shocking Education Gap for American Children*. New York: Mariner Books; Reprint edition.

Hove, M.J. & Risen, J.L. (2009). It's all in the timing: Interpersonal synchrony increases affiliation, *Social Cognition*, 27(6), 949–960.

Israel, E.P. (2012). *Instructor Perception of el Sistema-Based Programs in the United States*. Unpublished thesis, M Arts (Arts Management), Faculty of the College of the Arts and Sciences, American University, Washington, DC.

Koutsoupidou, T. & Hargreaves, D. (2009). An experimental study of the effects of improvisation on the development of children's creative thinking in music, *Psychology of Music*, 37(3), 251–278.

MacDonald, R., Kreutz, G. & Mitchell, L. (2012). *Music, Health and Well-Being*. New York: Oxford University Press.

Miksza, P. (2010). Investigating relationships between participation in high school music ensembles and extra-musical outcomes: An analysis of the education longitudinal study of 2002 using bio-ecological development model, *Bulletin of the Council for Research in Music Education*, 186, 7–25.

NfER (2000). Arts education in secondary school: Effects and effectiveness. https ://www.nfer.ac.uk/media/1681/eaj01.pdf (accessed 1st April 2020).

Oecd (2019). *PISA 2018, Results Combined Executive Summaries, Volume i, ii & iii*. PISA, Paris: OECD Publishing. https://www.oecd.org/pisa/Combined_Executive_Summaries_PISA_2018.pdf.

Ofsted (2019). Education Inspection Framework, Her Majesty's Print, London. https://assets.publishing.service.gov.uk/government/uploads/system/upl

oads/attachment_data/file/801429/Education_inspection_framework.pdf (accessed 1st April 2020).

Rabinowitch, T.C., Cross, I. & Burnard, P. (2012). Musical group interaction, intersubjectivity and merged subjectivity. In: D. Reynolds & M. Reason (eds) *Kinaesthetic Empathy in Creative and Cultural Practices*. Bristol: Intellect Press.

Saarikallio, S. (2006). *Differences in adolescents' use of music in mood regulation*. 9th International Conference on Music Perception and Cognition, Bologna, Italy.

Schellenberg, E.G. (2014). Musical and nonmusical abilities. In: G.E. McPherson (ed.) *The Child as Musician: A Handbook of Musical Development*. 2nd ed. Oxford, UK: Oxford University Press.

Sloboda, J., Lamont, A. & Greasley, A. (2009). Choosing to Hear Music. In: S. Hallam, I. Cross & M. Thaut (eds) *The Oxford Handbook of Music Psychology*. OUP. https://doi.org/10.1093/oxfordhb/9780198722946.013.42.

Small, C. (1998). *Musicking: The Meanings of Performing and Listening*. Connecticut: Wesleyan University Press.

Strait, D. L., and Kraus, N. (2014). Biological impact of auditory expertise across the life span: Musicians as a model of auditory learning. *Hear. Res.*, 308, 109–121.

Wright, R., Davies, B. & Davies, B. (2010). Class, power, culture and the music curriculum. In: R. Wright (ed.) *Sociology and Music Education* (pp. 57–72). Routledge. https://doi.org/10.4324/9781315087856-14

Yang, H., Ma, W., Gong, D., Hu, J. & Yao, D. (2014). A longitudinal study on children's music training experience and academic development, *Scientific Reports*, 4, 5854.

10

Vision-driven curriculum practices
'Deeply Christian, serving the common good'

Andy Wolfe, Caryn Smith, Lisa Harford and Mark Lacey

Introduction

Most schools have clear statements of their vision, mission or values. Significant attention has been given to the importance of such vision and values both in education (Leithwood et al., 2006; Puusa et al., 2013) and within other sectors of public life (Collins, 2001). While many writers are positive about the impact of leaders' values and moral purpose on student outcomes (for example, Day and Gu, 2018), others are less confident; for example, Coates highlighted examples of "an often uncertain journey from print to practice" and "badge engineering" (2017: 91, building on Coates, 2015) where a disconnect between vision and practice may be observed.

These mission statements can sometimes appear blurry and interchangeable in schools but typically centre around public declarations of core principles, often using key words or phrases. Lumby and English noted the importance of the language used by leaders, "Language and leadership are inseparable. Leaders traffic in language. It is language that defines problems and solutions" (2010: 1). The key words are sometimes combined into wider notions of 'culture', helpfully defined by Schein as,

> a pattern of shared basic assumptions that the group learned as it solved its problems of external adaptation and internal integration, that has worked well enough to be considered valid and therefore, to be taught to new members as the correct way to perceive, think and feel in relation to those problems.
>
> *(Schein 2010: 17)*

The school's vision is outworked by the choices made by leaders and evidenced by noticeable behaviours that are typically undertaken or rejected by agents within it.

Coates argues that such statements "must become reference points for decision-making, strategic intent, evaluation and organisational dialogue" (2017: 95).

Regardless of their stated 'why', and whether vision is seen as an individual, social or cultural construct, there are metrics by which schools' effectiveness is judged. Many of these metrics are imposed and universal yet frequently changing in nature. Two major inspection schedules have recently moved towards focusing on the impact of a school's vision on its outcomes. Both presuppose, to some extent, a theoretical construct that a school's intent or vision will have a significantly positive effect on pupil outcomes. They evaluate the impact of leaders' decision-making on a wide range of school issues, focused particularly on the curriculum. While schools retain autonomy for the authorship and identity of their vision, this chapter seeks to explore the impact of a national vision on a large group of schools, firstly by outlining that vision and its potential implications for curriculum development, and then spotlighting two examples where this is being put into practice: firstly in a primary school and, secondly, across a medium-sized multi-academy trust (MAT).

The pursuit of vision takes an expansive perspective on aims and is likely to move beyond standard accountability requirements, drawing on the depth of an individual's, or a society's, search for meaning and meaningful life. This Christian vision for education, amongst other faiths, offers a response to the human search for meaning and enables schools to provide a curriculum that seeks to walk alongside children as they explore the meanings, possibilities and purposes for their lives.

'Why' not just 'what'

The Church of England began opening schools in its parishes in 1811 under the now somewhat antiquated title 'The National Society for Promoting the Education of the Poor'. The schools became the first 'free at the point of use' schools in England, seeking social justice through improved access and expansion of opportunity to learn beyond families who could pay for education. They established themselves quickly, linking strongly with local churches and standing at the heart of communities across the country. There are now around 4500 Church of England primary schools across England (accounting for 24% of primaries nationally, which rises steeply to around 70% of schools in a rural/small schools context), educating approximately 1 million children each day. From its inception, the 'why' of the education provided to serve these communities has shaped the schools' identity, purpose and provision, acting as an influential voice within the wider discourse at the local and national level.

Although there have been many articulations of this purpose throughout this history, the most recent was published in 2016, entitled 'The Church of England Vision for Education: Deeply Christian, Serving the Common Good', which was written by a group of educationalists, academics and theologians and chaired by

Professor David Ford (Regius Professor of Divinity, University of Cambridge) under the leadership of The Revd. Nigel Genders (Chief Education Officer). The Vision seeks to define the 'why' of education rather than simply the 'what' and offers an aspirational and inclusive vision for education for all schools, not just those run by the Church of England. The Vision for Education takes John 10:10 as its central text – 'Life in all its fullness' and is shaped around four key ideas (Figure 10.1).

These elements are explored in layers of multiple depths, beginning with an inclusive overview, followed by a theological underpinning of the terms and their practical application in education, drawing on a wide range of biblical thinking. The Vision has been warmly welcomed and embraced by school leaders, illustrating the importance of defining the core purpose of education, and seeing it as fundamental to effective leadership development and school improvement. While its carefully-written text warrants full reading, the four key ideas can be summarised as:

- **Educating for wisdom, knowledge and skills** – Fostering discipline, confidence and delight in seeking wisdom and knowledge (including a healthy and life-giving tension between knowledge-rich and biblical wisdom curriculum approaches) and fully developing talents in all areas of life.
- **Educating for hope and aspiration** – Seeking healing, repair and renewal, coping wisely with things and people going wrong, opening horizons and guiding people into ways of fulfilling them.
- **Educating for community and living well together** – Ensuring a core focus on relationships, participation in communities and the qualities of character that enable people to flourish together.
- **Educating for dignity and respect** – Ensuring the basic principle of respect for the value and preciousness of each person, treating each person as a unique individual of inherent worth.

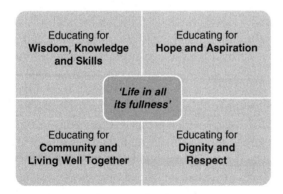

Figure 10.1 Overview of The Church of England Vision For Education: 'Deeply Christian, Serving the Common Good' (Church of England Office, 2016)

The Vision is not intended as a blueprint to be imposed on schools but rather offers an opportunity for school leaders to gather around a national identity and through the sharing of common language and interdependent conversation in order to develop a clearer sense of purpose and foundational thinking. This approach has engaged a wide variety of community and independent schools who are increasingly interested in this inclusive way of thinking about the core purpose of education. Through the programmes, networks and research of the Church of England Foundation for Educational Leadership, a body of resources has been developed to help leaders and teachers bring the Vision alive in their own context. These activities are entitled 'Ethos Enhancing Outcomes' and are based on Socratic questioning and coaching models equipping teachers and leaders to think through together the implications of vision for a wide range of school leadership issues, including curriculum development.

At the heart of the vision is the pursuit of human flourishing – applied to both adults and children: for where there are few flourishing adults, there will be few flourishing children. This is an aspirational goal for the curriculum, which goes far beyond any reductionist approach towards simply improving academic outcomes. The vision for 'life in all its fullness' offers a different perspective on the pressure that school leaders can feel under to make an artificial binary choice between academic rigour and the wellbeing or character development of their pupils. Indeed, the development of character is fundamental to any serious pursuit of sustained improvement in academic outcomes and is central to excellent learning experiences within the classroom.

The notion of human flourishing draws significantly on Aristotle and especially on his conception of *eudaimonia*. The meaning of *eudaimonia* can be traced etymologically from its roots of 'eu' (good) and 'daimon' (spirit) and refers to the notion of human flourishing. The concept can be considered from a number of viewpoints including physical flourishing (such as food, drink, exercise, health and rest); emotional flourishing (such as the consideration of our desires, feelings and reactions); societal flourishing (living well together, in relation to others, in community) and fourthly, flourishing in terms of personal creativity, self-expression and knowledge seeking. At its heart, human flourishing of children and adults requires not merely the presence or understanding of good character but actual activity or outworking through real examples of the virtues in action in the curriculum.

Educating for wisdom, knowledge and skills

The knowledge discourse has occupied a significant proportion of recent thinking about education, and has arguably become the dominant paradigm for curriculum development. While one could argue this has been fueled by the Gove curriculum and assessment reforms in the early part of this decade, the communication, acquisition, usage and recall of knowledge has been a mainstay of the education system for centuries. However, there are limitations to seeing this as the only way to think about curriculum – using 'knowledge-rich', 'knowledge-based', 'knowledge-centred' epithets. To expand this discourse, the Vision draws on the ancient concept of wisdom. While wisdom is a core element of much of the biblical narrative, there is of course no religious monopoly on the word, with its implications for synthesis of information, decision-making, ethical reflection and creativity quite clearly part of other approaches. This includes, for example, Aristotle's concept of *phrónesis* (or 'practical wisdom') within the virtue ethics discourse. It is a process that is fundamental to most human existence, including basic survival (food, warmth, safety and so on), relationships (parenting, family, friendship) and employment (ethics, values, problem solving, communication). All of these key elements have clear knowledge requirements but effective human living is characterised beyond knowledge and draws in wisdom, both conceptually and practically.

In order to enhance our pursuit of knowledge and to deepen our pupils' learning experience, it is helpful to consider the symbiotic tension between knowledge and wisdom. This might involve taking a given subject and considering the fundamental knowledge requisite for the scheme of learning but then considering more broadly the wisdom we are seeking to impart which, in many ways, could be seen as surrounding or underpinning that knowledge. We could consider a range of worked examples of this – for instance, the wisdom to apply artistic knowledge or technique to respond in oil paint with genuine creativity to a stimulus; the wisdom to evaluate whether contemporary European history is actively seeking to learn lessons from its own conflict and division-centred past, or the wisdom to inspire children to become ethical entrepreneurs who lead political or economic responses to climate change and dwindling earth resources.

Educating for hope and aspiration – beginning with imagination

Professor Michael Young defines the curriculum as an 'entitlement to knowledge' (2013: 23) and a 'guarantor of equality' (2013: 71). Drawing on Paulo Freire's notions of empowerment, emancipation and liberation, Young argues that curriculum processes can enact and encourage social justice. This can be achieved through recognition of the core role of reading in accessing the wider curriculum, for example, or building learning around episodic visits and cultural experiences not usually experienced by children outside the school context. Strong evidence for this approach is outlined by the Education Endowment Foundation's influential *Subject to Background* paper (EEF, 2017) with its strong focus on reading for pleasure, out-of-classroom learning and enrichment activities. Liberating curriculum thinking is built on giving access to what Young calls 'powerful knowledge'. A hopeful curriculum enacted by hopeful teachers has the potential to create ambitious opportunities for all children regardless of their starting point. This has significant implications for the 'hopefulness' associated with curriculum practices like ability grouping (and any resultant limitations placed on pupils due to grouping) as argued in Professor Becky Francis's *Grouping Study* (Francis et al., 2018). While the study stops short of calling time on setting, it highlights the lack of compelling data to support the practice and offers a wide range of useful practical questions to consider, whether schools group by ability or not.

Secondly, a note on imagination in curriculum and the ability to envision a future not yet known for the pupils in one's care. Theologian Walter Brueggemann writes: "The imagination must come before the implementation. Our culture is competent to implement almost anything and imagine almost nothing. It is our vocation to keep alive the ministry of imagination" (2001: 8–9). While it can be easily squeezed out of the pedagogical craft, the imagination of a child has immense potential and is there for the teacher to encourage, refine and cheer on. A curriculum that educates for hope and aspiration may do well to choose imagination as its first step.

Educating for community and living well together

A contemporary tendency to individualise or personalise learning has many merits but opens a danger where we see the curriculum as an individual rather than shared pursuit. This has implications for relationship building in classrooms, across and between schools. In seeking to support children's holistic development, this aspect of the Church of England Vision opens up the notion of character education. The Jubilee Centre's *Framework for Character Education* sets out a clear definition of character education and places an emphasis on the development of virtues in moral development and ethical decision-making:

> Character education includes all explicit and implicit educational activities that help young people develop positive personal strengths called virtues … Students need to decide wisely the kind of person they wish to become and to learn to choose between already existing alternatives or to find new ones. In this process, the ultimate aim of character education is the development of good sense, or practical wisdom; the capacity to choose intelligently between alternatives.
>
> *(Jubilee Centre, 2017: 2)*

Following a 2017 joint project with the Jubilee Centre for Character and Virtues, the Church of England Foundation for Educational Leadership published *Leadership of Character Education*, which outlines a wide variety of ways that schools can embed character education within their curriculum and leadership processes. Within the report, the role of character education is regarded as:

- seeking to develop and celebrate the flourishing of individuals, communities, families and societies;

- fundamental to the pursuit of academic excellence;
- taught implicitly through role-modelling and relationship, and taught through the deliberate embedding of leadership virtues in staff teams;
- central to a Christian vision for education for 'life in all its fullness';
- an investment in a legacy far beyond the school gates, impacting young people as friends, neighbours, parents, team members and employees.

(Church of England Foundation for Educational Leadership, 2017: 15)

This seeks to remove a false dichotomy between character and achievement, recognising that the most life-giving approaches to curriculum give space and experience to character development. There are numerous ways across every subject that character can be developed, while the focusing on learning together and quality relationships is key to an effective classroom where children feel inspired and permitted to progress together.

Educating for dignity and respect

The words 'dignity' and 'respect' are easily misunderstood as simply treating people well or properly. While courtesy and politeness are excellent qualities, dignity in learning is much deeper. However, we see teaching with dignity as *a pre-cursor to learning*. If the curriculum is appropriately challenging, pupils will try (and sometimes fail at) new things in lessons rather than repeating what they can already do. This carefully-gauged challenging is manifested both in curriculum thinking (which can create appropriate scenarios for challenge and possible failure) and also in pedagogy (which recognises the importance of enabling pupils to pursue, embrace and learn from failure). The importance of failure in learning is outlined in a range of writing from influential American psychologist Carol Dweck, whose work centres on the importance of developing a 'growth mindset' (see, for example, Dweck, 2016). The only way that this can happen in the classroom is through teachers establishing pedagogical approaches which support dignity and by the structural considerations of the curriculum. This could play out in a variety of ways – including, for example, pursuing persistence in problem-solving, risk-taking in performance, courage in writing style, experimentation in art – all of these would be sought by a great teacher, and all require dignity to be enacted.

As we argued, the Church of England Vision for Education helps open up the 'why' not just 'what' questions of curriculum design and implementation; however, it is not intended as a blueprint to be replicated in every school. Rather, school leaders are encouraged to use and interpret it, bringing it to life for their children in their own specific context. We now turn to look at two contrasting but complementary examples of organisations responding to the Vision document. In the first, headteacher Lisa Harford and deputy headteacher Caryn Smith outline their school's curriculum approach and its developing resonance with the Vision. In the second, Mark Lacey, a MAT chief executive, explains how his MAT's 15 academies work together as part of a peer support network to collaborate on curriculum design and process using the Vision document as a stimulus for discussion.

'Lived not laminated' – St James Church of England Primary School, Cheltenham, Lisa Harford and Caryn Smith

Our curriculum is underpinned by our aim to provide our community of children, staff and parents with a toolkit to thrive and lead life to the fullest both now and in the future. We have transformed our approach to teaching and learning and renovated our curriculum so that our ethos is core to all that we do. We have achieved this by weaving together our understanding of spiritual growth, the National Curriculum and the Church of England's Vision for Education so that the themes of wisdom, hope, community and dignity equip the children with the skills to live 'life in all its fullness' (John 10:10).

We decided that spiritual growth had to be at its core, complementing our Christian values and underpinning our philosophy of teaching. Staff worked hard together to unpick what spirituality meant to them, how it could be seen and how people could deepen their inner spirituality through a curriculum rich in experience and reflection. Central to our wheel is our school community and simply being human. Whether you are of faith or not we are all spiritual and have an innate desire to pursue the meaning of big questions: 'Who am I?', 'Why am I here?', 'What do I desire?' and 'How then shall I live?' Opportunities to explore these questions of life have been central to our curriculum design (Figure 10.2).

As a school, we live through our 12 core Christian values which are integral to our curriculum and school life and are part of our daily language. Within each curriculum theme, two values are explored and used continually to enhance pupils' development. They are threaded through our work and our planning cycle enables them to be revisited and built upon together with a shared language but with different contexts. As a result, the children's understanding grows as they move through the school; their language becomes more sophisticated as they make stronger connections between their life and biblical and ethical teachings; they are enabled to understand how to grow and flourish, academically, spiritually, morally, socially and culturally.

We believe we grow through creativity, curiosity, stillness and engagement with big questions. When planning as a year group, these are used to drive learning so that everyone has the opportunity to reflect on their own beliefs that inform their perspective on life; has a respect for different people's faith, feelings and values and gains enjoyment and understanding of the world that they live in.

The outer ring of our wheel symbolises our vision for our pupils. Through designing a curriculum with spiritual growth at the heart, we strive for our pupils

Figure 10.2 Curriculum Overview: St James Church of England Primary School, Cheltenham

to leave St James and enter the next part of their journey having been 'inspired and grown for fullness of life', with a stronger sense of identity, purpose and wisdom, being able to take on challenges and to show empathy towards others.

The spiritual wheel informs our practice and ultimately our approach to teaching and relationships across the school – it is our school's heartbeat. It is not differentiated for different ages nor is it progressively difficult; instead, we appreciate that this journey will be different for everyone.

Wisdom, hope, community and dignity are the cornerstones of our curriculum and are lived out through our spiritual wheel, as described in Table 10.1.

As a school, we now have a curriculum that supports the growth of the children through meaningful and relevant themes and considered drivers. It permeates through all aspects of school life and promotes our aim of fullness of life for

Table 10.1 The cornerstones of St James' Church of England Primary School curriculum

Wisdom, knowledge and skills	Clear teaching principles and a broad **curriculum** which enables pupils to learn new knowledge and skills, encourages curiosity and build on their understanding through making connections and manipulating and sharing their learning and **taking risks**.
	'Philosophy-For-Children' teaches the skills to debate and consider the knowledge they are given and ponder **big questions** with **honesty** and **courage**.
	Our Christian Values give our children a deep understanding of morality and how Jesus wants us to live our life. Time for **stillness** allows us to reflect on the power of our values.
	Children are taught to think critically, **creatively**, collaboratively and caringly; to nurture a **love** of the world and to develop and grow as individuals with a unique moral code steeped in humility and **responsibility**.
Hope and aspiration	Through our curriculum drivers: community, courageous advocacy and charity, our themes are developed so that in turn, children experience the benefits of giving, caring and creating in relation to our values. This work builds **relationships** and **co-operation**.
	Children, through a carefully crafted curriculum, are encouraged to value the school and wider environment and want the world to be the best that it can be allowing them to have a **sense of empathy** and develop their own **sense of identity**.
	Our nurturing ethos encourages our children to cope with set-backs, see mistakes as learning opportunities and helps them to develop their physical, mental and spiritual wellbeing.
Community and living well together	Jesus teaches us to love God and to love our neighbours as ourselves – we collaborate with other primary schools, including DGAT, secondary schools, Balcarras Teaching partnership, Gloucestershire University and our local church. We feel that these links greatly enrich our school and help to give our school a stronger **sense of identity**.
	We welcome visits from key individuals (e.g. emergency services, doctors, councillors, business leaders, charities, etc.) serving our locality to reinforce the schools' position within the **community**.
	Our school encourages participation, collaboration and a strong sense of community and we encourage our children and families to carry our vision and values outward into their local community and onward into their future lives. We aim to develop individuals who are **generous** and **trustworthy**.
Dignity and respect	We **respect** others and ourselves, cherish **friendship** all of which we develop through our development of spiritual growth. We recognise that 21st century Britain is enormously diverse. All members of the school understand that everyone within our school community should be respected equally, treated with **dignity** and shown **forgiveness**.

everyone. Through our exciting, wide-ranging curriculum, the children have a variety of opportunities to flourish and are supported by a culture of celebrating talent and nurturing aspiration.

'Embracing interdependence' – Diocese of Salisbury Academy Trust, Wiltshire, Mark Lacey

As part of its strategy to develop strong middle and senior leaders, the Diocese of Salisbury Academy Trust has engaged with the Church of England Foundation for Educational Leadership (CEFEL) to facilitate a peer support network across the Trust, focused on curriculum. Senior leaders from the 15 schools come together termly to develop practice around this shared leadership development priority, working inbetween these sessions in trios to visit and support one another's development. The approach has given these leaders a sense of identity, helping them to drive things at a whole school level and ensuring that they have had a prominent voice with their head teachers, governors and Trust representatives. A particular focus has been the potential impact of curriculum on the progress of disadvantaged pupils, with some schools serving communities where up to 45% of pupils are eligible for free school meals. Sessions have focused on the relationship between the Church of England's Vision for Education and curriculum development, with reference to wisdom, hope, community and dignity. The school leaders have been drawing on the question-based approach, 'Ethos Enhancing Outcomes' (CEFEL, 2018), and have been reflecting questions such as these:

- How would a visitor to your school know the values that underpin your curriculum decisions? How could they tell? What would they see? *(wisdom, knowledge and skills)*
- To what extent does your curriculum design 'open up horizons of hope and aspiration'? *(hope and aspiration)*
- Does your curriculum support the development of pupils' self-worth through experiences of success and celebration across a wide range of skills and talents? *(community and living well together)*
- How does your curriculum design 'pay special attention to the disadvantaged'? *(dignity and respect)*

The peer support network focuses on giving disadvantaged learners experiences to develop the capacity to learn in a way that diminishes differences with their peers. These children are less likely to make accelerated (or even expected) progress as they have not developed the skills they need for learning, specifically the ability to take risks, the resilience to cope with mistakes and the confidence to work collaboratively. Whatever a child's history, environment and experience, they are entitled to the same offer as all other pupils. This approach has thus focused on providing a wider range of learning experiences so that curriculum decisions can become an instrument of social justice within communities, thus bringing the idea of 'Educating for Hope and Aspiration' alive.

The bespoke curriculum offer for these children is tailored to provide exciting opportunities that allow pupils to develop new skills in safe environments. Each event requires children to work together, with relatively unknown others, to create something out of the ordinary. The engaging nature of the activities helps pupils to overcome their self-consciousness in such circumstances. The events are planned to cater for children of all ages, needs and genders, with a group from each school in the Trust. Pupils are carefully chosen based on the proposed activity – the opportunity may reflect their need for increased self-esteem or they may have a special interest or talent in this area to be built upon. Events have, for example, included creating movies on iPads (children with low self-esteem when communicating and those with speech and language difficulties) and coding robots and flying drones (children identified with ADHD or lower levels of concentration). All the events are held at one of the four hub schools and the adults chosen to lead are experienced in the related fields. Student leadership skills have also increased significantly, with some acting as 'digital leaders'.

Working collaboratively as a hub has enabled schools to broaden their curricula by working in partnership and to raise expectations of pupils in relation to communication and teamwork. It also allows utilisation of the talent within the teaching staff and the sharing of physical resources and technology across the hub, meaning each session has a greater 'wow' factor. As we have reflected on the nature of a hopeful curriculum, these experiences are making a significant contribution to children's aspirations and vision for their own future. This has engaged them well and improved motivation.

The Trust has been encouraged by the strong commitment from staff, parents and other stakeholders, and will now expand this work to include even more pupils. We have been delighted with the positive responses from pupils so far. We are also extending further opportunities for student leaders to take a more proactive role in teaching and facilitating sessions for others in the future.

A second aspect to the collaboration has focused on the impact of the Vision for Education in relation to mathematics pedagogy, again focused on the progress of disadvantaged pupils. Senior leaders have used the idea of 'Educating for Dignity and Respect' to re-shape teaching and learning, seeing dignity as a pre-cursor to learning. The Trust has worked hard with teachers and pupils to ensure that making mistakes is perfectly acceptable and that children's dignity is preserved when learning from errors. However, with these most vulnerable children, for whom success can often be difficult to achieve, this curriculum development increases their opportunities to succeed within a whole class context by providing them with a safe and respectful environment in which to overcome their most significant misconceptions before the key teaching input takes place. This approach is now becoming an integral part of the planning, teaching and learning process in all classes. As a result of this dignity-led teaching, teachers are reporting a change in pupils' attitudes in Maths, increased self-belief, strengthening of relationships, enjoyment of lessons and an upward trend in assessment scores. Equally, teachers themselves have reported feeling greater respect from colleagues, recognising the support that others have given and feeling that they can promote more of a shared responsibility towards outcomes at the end of the Key Stage. Equally, support staff feel part of the journey and there is real evidence of them feeling a sense of dignity about the work in which they are engaged.

'Called, connected, committed': implications for leadership development – Mark Lacey

The Church of England Foundation for Educational Leadership was set up in 2016 to develop inspirational leaders who are called, connected and committed to deliver the Church of England Vision for Education (CEFEL, 2016). It runs a wide range of programmes, networks and research for headteachers, middle and senior leaders, governors and MAT leaders. Many of these have taken a clear focus on curriculum development, and draw together groups of leaders to work on this shared leadership development priority. It is based on the Foundation's definition of 'connected':

> Leaders who are connected operate deliberately within communities of practice, positioning themselves within positive relationships that sustain and encourage all parties. They embrace interdependence, demonstrate compassion and embody service to others humbly. They create shared identity within their teams and draw colleagues around a common purpose.
>
> *(CEFEL, 2017: 27)*

Focusing on curriculum development is not a new idea for education; however, current changes in the Ofsted EIF are likely to bring it to the forefront of leaders' minds at all levels. Whilst recognising the opportunity this provides, we can also note the significant challenges presented for individual schools in meeting these new requirements. A significant number of peer support network groups are now running across England drawing schools together to share this developmental journey, putting the vision into practice. Some are focused on particular geographical areas while others bring particular kinds of schools together (for example, rural schools, secondary schools, MAT groups). These collaborative groups enable leaders to work on the crucial question of how their ethos is enhancing their outcomes – how they bring their vision alive in the day-to-day leadership decision making. This is clearly not unrelated to the Ofsted language of intent-implementation-impact. This convergence in thinking is potentially empowering to school leaders although there is also a recognition that the process of effective curriculum development rests on the leadership development skills of senior and middle leaders and classroom teachers.

However, we may choose to define our values, vision, ethos or purpose in school, the real test of a vision is the extent to which it is lived out in corridors and classrooms, in playgrounds and meetings – the extent to which it leads to rich, expansive and life-giving learning to which aspire in our schools nationally. Vision-driven curriculum development fosters confidence, delight and discipline in seeking wisdom, knowledge and skills, truth, understanding, and the know-how needed to shape life well. It opens up horizons of hope and aspiration, guiding pupils into ways of fulfilling them. It supports pupils in developing skills to cope wisely with things and people going wrong. It focuses on relationships, community and living well together, and the qualities of character that enable people to flourish together. It develops dignity and respect, focusing on what one needs to understand and to do in order to be a good person, citizen, parent, employee, team or group member or leader. To pursue this vision is only possible by starting with our 'why', not just our 'what', and then empowering leaders to think, collaborate and act together to bring the vision alive.

References

Brueggemann, W. (2001) *The Prophetic Imagination*. London: Fortress Press.

Coates, M. (2015) The co-operative: Good with schools? *Management in Education*, 29(1): 14–19.

Coates, M. (2017) Setting direction: Vision, values and culture. In: Earley, P. and Greany, T. (ed) *School Leadership and Education System Reform*. London: Bloomsbury.

Collins, J. (2001) *Good to Great*. New York: Harper Business.

Day, C. and Gu, Q. (2018) How successful secondary school principals in England respond to policy reforms: The influence of biography, *Leadership and Policy in Schools*, 17(3): 332–344.

Dweck, C. (2016) *Mindset: The New Psychology of Success - How We Can Learn to Fulfill Our Potential*. New York: Ballantine Books.

Education Endowment Foundation (2017) *Subject to Background*. https://educationendowmentfoundation.org.uk/evidence-summaries/evidence-reviews/ (accessed 1st April 2020).

Francis, B. Taylor, B., Hodgen, J., Tereshchenko, A, & Archer, L. (2018) *Dos and Don'ts of attainment grouping*. London: Institute of Education.

Jubilee Centre for Character and Virtues (2017) *A Framework for Character Education in Schools*. Birmingham: Jubilee Centre for Character and Virtues.

Leithwood, K., Day, C., Sammons, P., Harris, A. and Hopkins, D. (2006) *Successful School Leadership: What It Is and How It Influences Pupil Learning*. Nottingham: National College of School Leadership.

Lumby, J. and English, F. (2010) *Leadership as Lunacy and Other Metaphors for Educational Leadership*. Thousand Oaks, CA: Corwin.

Puusa, A., Kuittinen, M. and Kuusela, P. (2013) Paradoxical change and construction of identity in an educational organization, *Educational Management, Administration and Leadership*, 41(2): 165–178.

Schein, E. (2010) *Organizational Culture and Leadership*. San Francisco, CA: Jossey-Bass.

The Church of England Education Office (2016) Church of England vision for education: Deeply Christian, serving the common good. https://cofefoundati on.contentfiles.net/media/assets/file/Church_of_England_Vision_for_Edu cation_-_2016_jdYA7EO.pdf (retrieved 15/11/2019).

The Church of England Foundation for Educational Leadership (2017) Leadership of character education: Developing virtues and celebrating human flourishing in schools. https://cofefoundation.contentfiles.net/media /assets/file/CEFEL_LeadershipCharacter_Report_WEB.pdf (retrieved 15/11/2019).

Young, M., Lambert, D., Roberts, C. and Roberts, M. (2013) *Knowledge and the Future School: Curriculum and Social Justice*. London: Bloomsbury.

11

Oracy and the primary curriculum
What does research tell us?

Neil Mercer

Introduction

On the basis of my own research and that of many others, I have been talking to teachers about the functions of classroom talk and the role of spoken language in children's intellectual development for over 30 years. In recent times, two things have made this part of my work easier and more satisfying. First, the findings of research in such different fields as linguistics, psychology, neuroscience, sociology, anthropology and education have converged to provide a more coherent and convincing account of why the quality of children's talk experience in and out of school is of the utmost importance. The second is that I have found teachers – of all subjects, internationally, not just in the UK – increasingly aware of the relationship between children's language skills and their learning in school, and more interested in how research can help them take account of that relationship in their teaching. In this chapter, I will summarise what is now known, and what its implications are for teacher training and classroom practice.

Recently, a primary teacher told me that several children who had just joined her Reception class did not seem able to engage in any extended conversation, with her or with anyone else. This was not unusual in her experience, she remarked; but through her involvement with a local authority oracy initiative she now realised that it could be an indication of something more worrying than she had previously thought. She knew that some children lacked a rich language experience in their pre-school years, but had not realised the impact that this might have on their later linguistic and cognitive development. Her realisation reflected the findings of research in both the UK and the USA, which has shown that children who arrive at school with poor spoken language skills tend to make less progress academically, and this can continue even into their teens. This is certainly bad news. But as I said to her, and as I say to each new group of PGCE students as they begin their studies, the good news is that there are people can help those children transcend their destinies: their teachers. Children's futures can be changed if school provides them with a rich language experience and actively helps them develop the range of oracy skills they need for learning and communicating effectively with others.

Helping children to develop their language abilities will certainly enable them to participate more fully and successfully in school. Moreover, it will prepare them for the world of work and life in wider society. Many employers say that they want to recruit young people with good spoken communication skills, but that many school-leavers are not confident and able communicators. There is an increasing awareness amongst educational policy makers that oracy should figure amongst the '21st Century skills' that education systems should promote. The current situation is still some distance from where we need to be, which would be with oracy as a taught subject in the primary curriculum, just as 'literacy' and 'numeracy' already are; but some progress can be celebrated.

Spoken language has an additional significance for the quality of children's education beyond the development of children's communication skills, because talk is the principal medium for communication between teachers and their students. Overall, research evidence indicates that classroom education can be improved by focusing on the development of both teachers' and students' spoken language skills. Although they are closely related, I think it is useful to consider these two aspects (which can also be described as 'dialogic teaching' and 'oracy education') separately. Dialogic teaching is a set of talk-based strategies for teaching any subject, whether it be maths, history, English or whatever. Oracy education is the direct, explicit teaching of speaking and listening skills as part of the language and literacy curriculum, comparable to the direct, explicit teaching of algebra as part of mathematics. The case for each gives a special emphasis to the educational importance of talk which is lacking in traditional English curricula and traditional pedagogies; and dialogic teaching certainly requires teachers to have good oracy skills. They are two sides of the same coin; but they depend on different evidence bases and have different implications for policy and practice. I will discuss each in turn.

Dialogic teaching

Dialogic teaching is essentially a pedagogic approach which emphasises the importance of talk being used effectively for teaching and learning [1]. Its proponents argue that students, as well as teachers, need to be using talk actively to construct an understanding of curriculum content, rather than teachers only transmitting curriculum content and instruction through talk to an attentive, and largely silent, class. That this needs to be argued may seem strange to some, but in fact there has been some resistance to dialogic teaching by those attached to more traditional pedagogies, who use the apparent effectiveness of didactic teaching methods employed in other countries such as China to support their opposition. However, systematic research supports this approach. In a recent large-scale project carried out with my Cambridge colleagues Christine Howe and Sara Hennessy, we found that the ways teachers used spoken language and ensured the active participation of their students in classroom dialogue had direct, measurable effects on the academic success of their classes [2]. By analysing whole class and group-based interactions in 72 Year 6 classes in primary schools in southeast England, we found that teachers who engaged a high proportion of their students in discussing, explaining and asking questions about what they were learning enabled those students to get better SAT results than teachers who did not do so. Those teachers also sometimes withheld any evaluation of the responses made by students until several had been heard and the class had a chance to consider them; and they more frequently asked 'open questions' to which they did not know the answer (as well as the 'closed questions' teachers commonly used to test children's knowledge). Levels of attainment were also raised by teachers organising group work which we rated as well organised and productive (using criteria taken from the extensive research on group-based learning [3]). Moreover, the higher achieving classes also had more positive attitudes towards school. A parallel project at the University of York (of a similar large scale, funded by the Education Endowment Foundation and carried out by Robin Alexander and Frank and Jan Hardman) obtained similar positive results by training Year 5 teachers to use more 'dialogic' strategies in the classroom [4].

So what does this kind of dialogic teaching look like in practice? I will illustrate what I have described by using two transcripts of lessons from high-achieving classes in our Cambridge project. Transcript 1 is a Year 6 class which had been studying evaporation. The teacher first involved the children in a group-based activity in which they talked together to decide, as a group, whether they think each of a set of statements made by fictitious children about what happens to the water in a puddle is correct, incorrect or if they are unsure. The activity was based on two useful, research-based resources for planning group work: *Concept Cartoons* by Brenda Keogh and Stephen Naylor [5] and *Talking Points* by Lyn Dawes [6]. Such activities have been found to stimulate productive group discussion more effectively than giving children a set of questions about a topic. The teacher had introduced the activity as follows:

"So one child says, 'Puddles just dry up after the rain stops'; another child says, 'The water that used to be in the puddle is now in the clouds'. So, later on in the day, the puddle disappears. Where's it gone? This child thinks it's in the clouds. And the last child says, 'The water that used to be in the puddle is in the air'. Have a little chat on your table, who do you agree with? Anyone? What do you think?"

After this talk activity, the teacher led the children in a discussion about what the groups had decided; and the episode here come from that discussion. The 'pot' referred to contains the names of all the children, which the teacher used to randomly select children to contribute to the whole class discussion. In this way, she avoided picking just the most eager or knowledgeable. Names have been changed to maintain the anonymity of the teachers and their classes.

167

Transcript 1: evaporation

Teacher: Mmm. (*Moves to front of class. Speaks to class, counting on fingers*) 3, 2, 1. Right, I don't mind which statement you want to talk about. Maybe you agree with all of them, maybe you don't agree with any of them. Maybe you're not sure and maybe you heard someone say something on your table. Ahmed, kick us off.

Ahmed: I don't think any of them are correct, because puddles...I think one of them is correct, the first one, but it doesn't just dry straightaway when the rain stops. It went after a few days or a few hours.

Teacher: OK. But you don't think any of them are correct?

Ahmed: No.

Teacher: Who would like to build on or disagree with what Ahmed has said? (*Picks name stick from pot*) Raffy, what were you saying over on your table?

Raffy: (*Inaudible*).

Teacher: The water that used to be in the puddle is in the air?

Raffy: Yeah.

Teacher: Can you expand your idea, please?

Raffy: Erm...

Teacher: Do you want some help?

Raffy: Yeah.

Teacher: Ask someone on your table for help.

(*And a little later*)

Teacher: OK, so we've got someone that thinks none of them are correct; we've got someone that thinks that maybe the third one's correct, but she's not very sure. (*Picks another name stick out of pot*) Sally, what were you saying on your table?

Sally: We thought the second one was correct.

Teacher: You thought the second one was correct – 'the water that used to be in the puddle is now in the clouds'? And could you explain how you came to that conclusion? (*To Talim*) What's your explanation? Your explanation.

Talim: I think the puddle evaporates.

Teacher: You think the puddle evaporates? What does that word mean?

Talim: I think it's like, when you're in a sauna...

Teacher: When you're in a sauna, hmm mmm.

Talim: ...the water is too hot and it becomes cloudy inside.

Teacher: The water becomes cloudy inside the sauna? Keep going.

Talim: ...it becomes so hot that the water evaporates and goes up in the clouds.

Teacher: OK, do you know what, we've heard some really good ideas, and I think Talim might be on to something. But keep this in your head *(indicating interactive whiteboard).* We'll come back to it towards the end of the lesson and we'll see if we can decide a bit more firmly, because there's a lot of ideas in the room but there's not much certainty, and that's OK.

We can see the teacher here using some of the dialogic strategies that have been found to help children's educational progress. First, she based a groupwork exercise on a tried and tested type of activity, one which is likely to generate productive discussion. Then, in the whole class discussion, she encouraged several children to report back from their groups to share their views about the statements. She encouraged children to elaborate their views ('Can you expand that idea please?') and asked them to 'build on or disagree' with what they had heard. At the end of the discussion, she did not categorically endorse any views offered as correct or incorrect, but asked them to 'keep this in their heads' until the end of the lesson, when they would 'decide a bit more firmly' what was correct (which indeed they did).

Overall, research evidence suggests that teachers who balance clear, authoritative instruction with well-structured, interactive discussion in both small groups and whole classes are the most successful in ensuring that curriculum knowledge is understood and remembered. I should make it clear that the evidence does not suggest that teachers should avoid making clear instructional presentations to their classes, or that students should be encouraged to talk at length throughout lessons. Sometimes children will learn best if they sit quietly and listen. It is rather that successful teachers maintain a strategic balance between instructing a class of attentive students and giving them opportunities to express their thoughts and learn collaboratively. When teachers know what students know and do not know – what they understand and what they do not – they are better able to teach them. And it should be noted by any who are sceptical of the value of dialogic teaching that there have been no systematic classroom-based studies, small or large scale, which support the view that maintaining a highly traditional, monologic instructional approach gets the best results.

Oracy education

Teachers know that unproductive talk in class can waste time; it is important to stress that introducing oracy into school does not mean allowing more time in school for casual, idle chat. However, any behaviour regime or teaching approach that simply limits the opportunities for productive talk to happen in school is ignoring the research evidence, and so is seriously misguided. Two researchers and teacher trainers who are former primary teachers have expressed this very clearly:

> A neglect of the teaching of oracy is a recipe for continuing inequality and consolidating disadvantage. Teachers know this, but they are obliged to teach things

which can be marked according to measurable criteria such as spelling, grammar and punctuation, and certain mathematical operations. Children need to talk if they are to read well; they need to talk and read to stimulate thinking, and they need to think for themselves in order to write creatively and effectively.

(further evidence can be found in Dawes & Sams [6])

A focus on oracy means teaching every child the presentational, discussion and listening skills they need to handle a wide range of situations, how to work well in a group, how to share their ideas with the whole class, how to make a formal presentation and – last but not least – how to listen well and capture the essence of what they hear in an appreciative but critical way.

I mentioned above that one factor that has been shown to help children's learning is their participation in well-organised, productive groupwork. I noted that such groupwork needs to be based on suitable activities; but it is also the case that group discussion is only likely to be productive if children are taught *how* to conduct a reasoned discussion. We cannot assume that the kind of language use involved is already part of the talk repertoire of primary school children. They may never have heard a reasoned discussion at home, so how can they have learned how to participate in one? It is not so difficult to teach children how to do so. Classroom-based research has shown that one of the keys to achieving productive groupwork is to get the children to agree on a set of 'ground rules' when they talk and work together [7]. Also, sometimes known as 'discussion guidelines', these rules are the characteristics that research has shown to be typical of productive discussions across a range of collaborative learning and problem-solving situations. They generate the kind of interaction which is called 'Exploratory Talk', in which participants do not just interact, they *interthink* [8]. Over a period of time, such as a school term, the use of such ground rules can transform the quality of discussion in a class – and, as we have shown, help to develop the reasoning skills of individual children. An example of a set of ground rules created by a teacher with her class is shown in Figure 11.1.

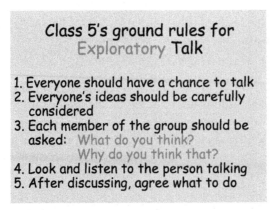

Figure 11.1 Ground rules for talk in groups

Transcript 2 illustrates the kind of interaction that is Exploratory Talk. Some weeks after their teacher has agreed with a set of 'ground rules for talk' with their class, three 11-year-old children are doing a computer-based activity about the Vikings. In the role of Viking invaders, they are planning a raid on the British coast, and have to use the information available to choose between a limited set of options for how to proceed.

Transcript 2: exploratory talk

Diana:	Let's discuss it. Which one shall we go for?
All:	(*inaudible – reading from instructions*)
Peter:	1 2 3 or 4 (*reading out the number of options available*) Well we've got no other chance of getting more money because.
Adrian:	And there's a monastery.
Diana:	And if we take number 2 there's that (*inaudible*).
Peter:	Yeh but because the huts will be guarded.
All:	Yeh.
Adrian:	And that will probably be guarded.
Diana:	It's surrounded by trees.
Peter:	Yeh.
Adrian:	And there's a rock guarding us there.
Peter:	Yes there's some rocks there. So I think I think it should be 1.
Adrian:	Because the monastery might be unguarded.
Diana:	Yes 1.
Adrian:	1 yeh.
Peter:	Yeh but what about 2? That, it might be not guarded. Just because there's huts there it doesn't mean it's not guarded does it? What do you think?
Diana:	Yes, it doesn't mean it's not. It doesn't mean to say it's *not* guarded does it. It may well be guarded I think we should go for number 1 because I'm pretty sure it's not guarded.
Adrian:	Yeh.
Peter:	OK, yes, number 1 (*he keys in 1*).

In Transcript 2, we are seeing three people interthinking. They share relevant information and reason about what to do. They question each other's ideas, but in the interests of achieving their joint goal, rather than asserting individual dominance, they ask each other what they think. They all participate and they achieve a consensus. As well as proving a good opportunity for children to develop the oracy skills required for effective teamwork, our research has shown that this kind of collective reasoning develops children's individual reasoning [8].

Regarding other aspects of oracy education, research suggests that presentational skills should be taught explicitly. Such skills may perhaps be expected to emerge indirectly through building children's social confidence, but evidence suggests that expressly teaching children how to use spoken language effectively is the key to developing their social confidence [9]. Innovative schools which have taken up oracy education, such as School 21 in the UK, have used methods which can be taken up and used by any teacher.

In order to help teachers recognise the range of skills which children need to develop to cope well with the variety of talk situations they will encounter in their lives, my colleagues Ayesha Ahmed, Paul Warwick and I worked with members of School 21 (with involvement of other schools and spoken language experts) to devise the Oracy Framework, which is now available on both the Cambridge University and Voice 21 websites[10, 11]. That framework can be used as a basis for assessing the skills of children in a class. Individuals will commonly be found to have different 'oracy profiles'. Some may be good at speaking in public, but not so effective when working in a group. Some may be good listeners but nervous speakers. Putting oracy into the curriculum can help them all achieve the confident capability they need for learning in school and for their future lives.

Overall, then, there is now a compelling body of research evidence to support the growing interest in oracy as both an aspect of pedagogy and a curriculum subject. It is vital that this interest in supporting childrens' spoken language development is not a transient initiative. Research tells us that children offered direct teaching of oracy skills and who are taught by teachers who have a suitable repertoire of dialogic teaching skills and methods are likely to learn more readily, remember what they have learned and be much better equipped to deal with life in wider society. Educational failure can follow from language deprivation in young children, and once ground − in terms of curriculum learning − has been lost, it becomes increasingly difficult for children to catch up. Oracy education should not be just for the privileged few in the private school sector. In the interests of every child, we must advocate the direct teaching of oracy, and the use of the kind of dialogic teaching which is supported by research evidence.

References

1. Mercer, N., Wegerif, R. & Major, L. (eds) (2019) *The Routledge International Handbook of Research on Dialogic Education.* Abingdon: Routledge.
2. Howe, C., Hennessy, S., Mercer, N., Vrikki, M. & Wheatley, L. (2019) Teacher-student dialogue during classroom teaching: Does it really impact upon student outcomes? *Journal of the Learning Sciences*, 4, 28. doi: 10.1080/10508406.2019.1573730.

3. Alexander, R.J. (2018) Developing dialogue: Genesis, process, trial, *Research Papers in Education*, 33(5). http://robinalexander.org.uk/wp-con tent/uploads/2019/12/RPIE-2018-Alexander-dialogic-teaching.pdf (accessed 1st April 2020).

4. Keogh, Brenda & Naylor, Stuart (1991) Concept Cartoons. See https:// www.millgatehouse.co.uk/concept-cartoons-research/.

5. Dawes, L. & Warwick, P. (2012) *Talking Points: Discussion Activities in the Primary Classroom*. Abingdon: David Fulton/Routledge.

6. Dawes, F. & Sams, C. (2017) *Talkbox: Activities for Teaching Oracy with Children Aged 4–8*. Abingdon: Routledge.

7. Mercer, N. (2019) *Language and the Joint Creation of Knowledge: The Selected Works of Neil Mercer*. Abingdon: Routledge. https://thinkingtogether. educ.cam.ac.uk (accessed 1st April 2020).

8. Littleton, K. & Mercer, N. (2013) *Interthinking: Putting Talk to Work*. Abingdon: Routledge.

9. Mercer, N. & Mannion, J. (2018) *Oracy Across the Welsh Curriculum: A Research-Based Review and Recommendations for Teachers*. Cambridge: Oracy Cambridge. https://oracycambridge.org/wp-content/uploads/2018 /07/Oracy-across-the-Welsh-curriculum-July-2018.pdf (accessed 1st April 2020).

10. https://www.educ.cam.ac.uk/research/projects/oracytoolkit/oracyskillsf ramework/ (accessed 1st April 2020).

11. https://www.voice21.org/our-resources (accessed 1st April 2020).

12

Unlocking research
To new possibilities

James Biddulph and Julia Flutter

In 1981, Lawrence Stenhouse, educationalist and visionary, is said to have said that teachers will change the world of the school by understanding it. Throughout this book, we have met teachers and researchers who are stepping across the research–practice divide to unlock the transformative potential of research-informed professional knowledge: they are trying to understand it. Individually, each of our chapter authors has shaped a piece for our patchwork which, when placed alongside those of others, enables us to see the patterns of possibility that are brought to light when evidence and practice become woven together.

Teachers as research consumers

Our contributors' stories reveal their own, differing reasons for setting out on their journeys of discovery and each practitioner has developed a unique approach to using research evidence. For some, an interest in research was a springboard in which research findings stimulated new ideas, new directions or an impetus for change. One example can be found in Rachel, Lucy and Harriet's Chapter 5 where conclusions drawn from developmental psychology research inspired and informed their innovations for a play-based curriculum in Key Stage 1. In other cases, we saw how theories and evidence drawn from research literature provided a framework of principles to guide curriculum decision-making; an example of this type of approach is Richard and Emilie's Chapter 6, which describes how the principles of harmony education underpin the school's coherent curriculum framework. Beyond its role in helping to answer the 'how' and 'what' questions of curriculum design, research and theory can also support thinking about the 'why' questions with respect to values, aims and purposes. In Chapters 8 and 10, we saw how some faith schools are using research to explore ways of connecting pedagogical approaches to their curricular aims. Likewise, Chapter 9, written by Phil, Michelle and Luke, evidences how an intuitive belief in the power of music was strengthened by looking to research; in doing so, they have a stronger discourse to argue their case and position.

Teachers as researchers

As well as being end users of published research, teachers are increasingly producers of research findings in their own right, whether in collaboration with external researchers, in school-based networks or within their own classrooms. The University of Cambridge Primary School, the first University Training School of its kind in the UK, has a mission that describes the concept of the teacher as researcher – not necessarily leading large-scale research projects (yet), but as a minimum starting point to develop a researcher mindset, asking: "have we done everything possible to understand how to help each child flourish in a kind and inclusive community?" Teacher research offers a useful way to monitor and evaluate new initiatives, enabling teachers to know whether strategies are proving effective or not. Action research cycles and spirals are commonly used to implement, test and refine new initiatives in primary schools. Classroom observation is another, long-established tool for giving feedback on practice and can be a valuable way of prompting new thinking and reflection. If the reader has enjoyed this book, the second in our series will introduce different professional development and learning that has replaced traditional 'monitoring and appraisal-linked observation' that can take place in schools. Gathering a broad range of data on pupil attainment allows teachers to build a clear, detailed picture of pupils' progress and creates a holistic, systematic process that allows assessment *for* learning, rather than simply *of*, learning (Wiliam, 2009). Teacher research communities and networks are springing up in England and other countries, fostering exchanges of classroom-based research findings and building teachers' confidence in engaging with research and researching. This groundswell of interest in research is heartening but enthusiasm for building bridges between research and practice is not universal or without controversy.

A bridge too far?

A quick trawl of the social media site, Twitter, reveals the disquiet that some teachers and researchers feel about teachers engaging with, and in, research and we must acknowledge that unlocking research can place some additional demands on teachers. The most common complaint is time. With workload pressures placing huge loads on teachers' working hours, it is reasonable to ask the question, "Why is it worth adding research to the long list of teacher responsibilities?" One answer to this is that research and theory can be used to inform our understanding of how children learn best and which pedagogical approaches are most effective; this knowledge will necessarily save time, energy and resources being spent on doing things that are ineffective. However, Lawrence Stenhouse, whose words opened this chapter, pointed to a deeper reason why research engagement is necessary for teachers. He argued that teachers' professional knowledge should be built on a synergy between research and practice, requiring every teacher to have:

- The commitment to systematic questioning of [his or her] own teaching as a basis for development.
- The commitment and the skills to study [his or her] own teaching.
- The concern to question and to test theory in practice (1975: 143).

These commitments are not proposed as externally imposed directives or short-term initiatives but instead they are put forward as being the characteristic dispositions that a professional in almost any field could be expected to hold. It is also important to acknowledge that being a member of a profession implies a shared commitment to certain values, behaviours and standards. As Canadian educationalists Michael Fullan and Andy Hargreaves point out, a willing compliance to shared professional principles and continued professional learning lay:

> at the heart of an effective and continuously growing teaching profession and, in turn, the best visions and versions of it are rooted firmly in a system culture of collaborative professionalism that cultivates individual and collective efficacy.
>
> *(2016: 2)*

Research unlocked

As we have seen throughout this book, inviting teachers to unlock the door between research and practice opens up new pathways for professional knowledge. However, as many teachers and researchers will recognise, moving from theory to practice often allows polarities to emerge, which can cause confusion and lead to spurious divisions. Familiar encampments in education are the so-called 'traditionalist' and 'progressive' approaches to teaching and, in relation to the curriculum, there is the ongoing debate between skills-based and knowledge-based learning. Faced with this panoply of diverse theories, evidence and ideas, how can teachers navigate beyond the unlocked door? For an answer to this important question, we need to travel back in time to ancient Greece and be guided by the thinking of philosopher and educator Aristotle.

Aristotle wrote of three forms of knowledge – *techne, episteme* and *phronesis* – and each of these three forms is essential to our understanding and our ability to make reasoned judgments and actions, as Canadian researchers Elizabeth Kinsella and Allan Pitman explain:

> *Phronesis* is generally defined as practical wisdom or knowledge of the proper ends of life. In Aristotle's scheme, *phronesis* is classified as one of several "intellectual virtues" or "excellences of mind" (Eikeland, 2008). Aristotle (trans.

1975) distinguished *phronesis* from the other two virtues of *episteme* and *techne*. In Aristotle's conception, drawn from Flybjerg (2001), *episteme* is characterised as scientific, universal, invariable context-independent. The original concept is known today through the terms epistemology and epistemic. *Techne* is characterised as context-dependent, pragmatic, variable, craft knowledge and is oriented toward practical instrumental rationality governed by a conscious goal. The original concept appears today in terms such as technique, technical and technology. *Phronesis*, on the other hand, is an intellectual virtue that implies ethics. It involves deliberation that is based on values, concerned with practical judgement and informed by reflection. It is pragmatic, variable, context-dependent and oriented toward action.

(2012: 2)

We believe that Aristotle's ideas can lead us forward beyond the unlocked door. Following this new path requires that teachers, individually and collectively as a profession, engage with published research evidence and theory (*episteme*) and consider this knowledge alongside wisdom drawn from their expertise and experience of their own classrooms and contexts (*techne*); in combination, these two strands give rise to a range of differing possibilities for action and it is through the third strand (*phronesis*) – involving reflection and informed, ethical judgement – that action can be decided upon and taken.

Teachers in dialogue

It must also be acknowledged, however, that professional decision-making and autonomy in education (as in many other professions) is often infringed by external forces such as policy and the prevailing economic conditions. Our new path can be quickly obstructed. Addressing this concern, Kinsella and Pitman argue that there are:

> two ways in which the knowledge derived from experience can lead: in the positive case, to a reflective practice of judgement based on a quest for wise practice and directed toward doing what is best; alternatively, to a practice grounded in fear, of doing what is safest from a self-interested and protectionist perspective. In other words, knowledge can lead one from doing what is morally responsible to doing only that for which one might be held accountable. Taking phronesis seriously as a significant form of professional knowledge holds potential for promoting the former, and for counterbalancing what seems to have become an emphasis on the latter, in professional practice.
>
> *(2012: 171)*

A further defence against these obstructions lies in professional collegiality. Maxine Greene writes that, "for those of us in education, it seems peculiarly important that both the critique and the vision of education be developed within and not outside what we conceive to be our learning community" (1995: 61). Professional bodies like the UK's newly established Chartered College of Teaching, which bears the Royal Charter for the teaching profession, offer a vital opportunity for collective phronesis, celebrating and curating of the professional knowledge of teachers.

In the curation offered in this book, the authors and editors have argued for the importance of professional dialogue as a key feature of curriculum design. Dialogue in professional learning is seen as plural and inclusive, emphasising the teacher's role in shaping (or inhibiting) learning opportunities for children *but* requiring professional agency and meta-level dialogue about dialogue (Alexander, 2020). In a post-truth world in which uncertainties prevail and in which clarity is often sought through social media, our professional duties must include more robust opportunities to deepen our understanding of the *ways we do our work*. A starting point, as can be seen throughout this book and indeed in the books yet to come in the Unlocking Research series, is to ask more and better questions. Through speaking and inviting questions, Paulo Friere talked about the need to move from abstract musings to concrete realities in which teachers find themselves. In a similar vein, John Dewey talked about knowledge as making a difference in and to things – of knowing as 'a change in reality' (Dewey, 1931: 54). Writing for the Chartered College of Teaching in 2019, Professor Colin Richards described Lawrence Stenhouse as the Chartered College's 'patron saint', and we close this book with a reminder of Stenhouse's words in advocacy of the professional agency of teachers which offer us a powerful, though as yet unfulfilled, declaration of intent. In this book, and the series of Unlocking Research, we also advocate the message that Stenhouse promotes; in the end teachers will change the world of the school by understanding it better (Stenhouse, 1981).

References

Alexander, R.J. (2020) 'Dialogic pedagogy in a post-truth world'. In: Mercer, N., Wegerif, R., & Major, L. (eds) *The Routledge International Handbook of Research on Dialogic Education*. Abingdon: Routledge.

Dewey, J. (1931) *Philosophy and Civilization*. New York: Minton, Balch and Company.

Fullan, M. & Hargreaves, A. (2016) *Bringing the Profession Back in: Call to Action*. Oxford, OH: Learning Forward.

Greene, M. (1995) *Releasing the Imagination: Essays on Education, the Arts and Social Change*. San Francisco, CA: Jossey-Bass.

Kinsella, E.A. & Pitman, A. (eds) (2012) *Phronesis as Professional Knowledge Practical Knowledge in the Professions*. Amsterdam: Sense Publishers.

Stenhouse, L.A. (1975) *An Introduction to Curriculum Research and Development.* London: Heinemann.

Stenhouse, L.A. (1981) What counts as research? *British Journal of Educational Studies*, 29(2): 103–114.

Wiliam, D. (2009) *Assessment for Learning: What, Why and How? Inaugural Professorial Lectures.* London: UCL IOE Press.

Afterword

Stephen J Toope

"I never let my schooling interfere with my education", Mark Twain allegedly remarked (Robinson, 1995). The quote may be apocryphal but it contains a kernel of truth; an education is more – much more – than what we are formally taught in class.

Twain's witticism came to mind while reading some of the authors in this volume discuss the process by which educators set out to design a curriculum. I was especially taken by attempts to define a curriculum not only as prescribed "content", but as a "lived experience". This approach acknowledges that, while built on shared values and a common knowledge base, a successful educational journey must at all times be open to – and indeed enriched by – the full diversity of life.

This ethos is embodied in the work of the University of Cambridge Primary School, which explicitly articulates its aims to be inclusive, to encourage achievement and to innovate in its practices. By asking not only what subject matter students will be taught, or how they will be examined, but what kind of people those students will turn out to be, it has developed a curriculum whose main focus is on nurturing "compassionate citizens".

What is true for primary or secondary education applies also to the area I am most familiar with – universities. In that context, openness means not only welcoming and celebrating the diversity of our students' backgrounds, but also embedding diversity of perspectives into the syllabus, and embracing new ways of teaching and assessing.

The University of Cambridge's own mission is to contribute to society through education, learning and research. Among its core values is the "encouragement of a questioning spirit", and the provision of an education that "enhances the ability of students to learn throughout life".

Even as we seek to prepare students for the future worlds of work, relationships and leisure, the truth is that we don't yet know what new challenges – technological, environmental, human – may emerge 10, 20 or 50 years from now. Despite its ubiquity, the World Wide Web was only invented in 1989. Who could have foreseen then the profoundly disruptive and transformative effect it has had on all aspects of our lives?

So curriculum design, from early years' settings and all the way through to life-long education, must not only take into consideration our societies' current needs, but also – to steal a coinage – prepare individuals to deal with the "unknown unknowns" that may emerge. As well as instilling aspiration and curiosity, we need educational journeys that will develop resilience and resourcefulness.

$$***$$

Every age has its challenges. It feels, however, as if we are living in times of remarkable complexity. This feeling is compounded by the unsettling pace of change, and by the global scale of the problems we are up against. It is further abetted by the rise of technologies that are able to connect us to others, but also to accentuate a sense of isolation and difference.

Awareness has been growing – partly due to the activism of school-age children around the world – about the finite nature of our natural resources. Climate change is real and dangerous. And as the world's weather patterns become ever more unstable, we are likely to see an increase in the number of climate refugees – adding to the already vast numbers of people displaced by conflict and poverty.

We are making inroads against infectious diseases, but are now faced with a world-wide increase in chronic diseases, though our confidence has been upended by the fast spread of COVID-19. We are still faced with a word-wide increase in chronic diseases, from cancer and diabetes to Alzheimer's and dementia. As populations grow, we are confronted by the challenge of ensuring sustainable food supplies, affordable and clean energy, proper sanitation and quality education for all.

Addressing global challenges of this magnitude will require creative and socially committed minds, equipped with the knowledge, skills and the inclination to think beyond the boundaries of intellectual disciplines. It will require minds that are able to grasp the diversity of perspectives and approaches.

Educators have an essential role to play in developing the curricula that will enable students to grow into engaged, open-minded citizens, prepared to contribute to society. Above all, they must arm students with the tools – intellectual, social and emotional – that will allow them to thrive in an ever-more complex world.

To paraphrase the old saying: give a student some knowledge, and she will use it for a day. Teach a student to create and apply the knowledge, and she will use it for life.

Reference

Robinson, F.G. (Ed.) (1995) *The Cambridge Companion to Mark Twain*. Cambridge: Cambridge University Press.

Index

Page numbers in *italics* indicate figures. Page numbers in **bold** indicate tables.

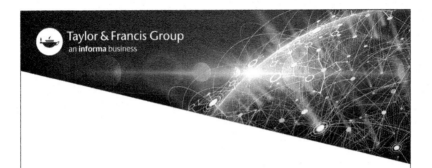